Writers & Critics

Chief Editor
A. Norman Jeffares

R. W. Noble

Joyce Cary

JOYCE CARY

Oliver & Boyd
Edinburgh

Oliver & Boyd

Croythorn House
23 Ravelston Terrace
Edinburgh, EH4 3TJ
(A Division of Longman Group Limited)

0 05 002579 1 Paperback
0 05 002580 5 Hardback

Printed in Great Britain by
Cox & Wyman Ltd, London, Fakenham and Reading

Contents

Contents

Acknowledgements

I am particularly grateful to Charles Peake (Reader in English, University of London) and Jennifer Breen (Lecturer in English, Polytechnic of North London), who read my typescript at various stages and made many valuable suggestions. I am also indebted to Barbara Hardy (Professor of English, University of London), Gerald Moore (Reader in Literature, University of Sussex), and Alida Noble for their useful comments on several chapters of my typescript.

I should also like to thank the following people: I. R. Willison (Editor, *New Cambridge Bibliography of English Literature*, IV), who showed me the proofs of his bibliography of Joyce Cary; Tristram Cary (who kindly provided the photograph upon which the cover design is based), Sir Michael Cary, and Winifred Davin, who answered queries about Joyce Cary's life; the staff of the Bodleian Library, who gave me access to Joyce Cary's MSS; A. W. R. Seward and Professor Jeffares, who gave editorial assistance.

Finally, acknowledgements are due to Michael Joseph Ltd for permission to quote extracts from their editions of Joyce Cary's works as follows: *Charley is My Darling, A House of Children, Herself Surprised, To be a Pilgrim, The Horse's Mouth, The Moonlight, A Fearful Joy, Prisoner of Grace, Except the Lord* and *Spring Song and Other Stories*. The passages from *Aissa Saved, An American Visitor, The African Witch, Castle Corner, Mister Johnson* and *Not Honour More* are reproduced by kind permission of the estate of Joyce Cary.

R.W.N.

Acknowledgements

Note

Abbreviated titles by which Joyce Cary's works are cited in references:

A.R.	*Art and Reality*
A.S.	*Aissa Saved*
A.V.	*An American Visitor*
A.W.	*The African Witch*
B.P.	*To Be a Pilgrim*
C.A.F.	*The Case for African Freedom and Other Writings on Africa*
C.C.	*Castle Corner*
C.I.M.D.	*Charley Is My Darling*
E.L.	*Except the Lord*
F.J.	*A Fearful Joy*
H.C.	*A House of Children*
H.M.	*The Horse's Mouth*
H.S.	*Herself Surprised*
M.	*The Moonlight*
M.J.	*Mister Johnson*
N.H.M.	*Not Honour More*
P.G.	*Prisoner of Grace*
P.M.	*Power in Men*
S.S.	*Spring Song and Other Stories*

The unpublished material cited in references is in the James Osborn Collection of Joyce Cary's papers in the Bodleian Library, Oxford.

1 Introduction

Joyce Cary's central achievement—*Mister Johnson* (1939), and the trilogy containing *Herself Surprised* (1941), *To Be a Pilgrim* (1942), and *The Horse's Mouth* (1944)—extended the form and matter of the English novel. Many contemporary British novelists, such as C. P. Snow and Evelyn Waugh, wrote traditional realism —the typical or comic in social and moral relations, expressed with conventional syntax and chronological narration. Cary drew on this long tradition of British realism in all his novels. But in his most significant fiction, notably *Mister Johnson* (1939) and *The Horse's Mouth* (1944), he integrated these conventions of realism with modernist methods, such as the stream-of-consciousness technique and present-tense narration, which emphasise man's inward condition. From this basis, Cary's important extensions to the art of fiction were, firstly, his form of trilogy which presents a triple view of partially coincidental lives and times, and secondly, the first valid novels about West African life to be written in English. My purpose is to illuminate the significance and quality of Cary's novels by concentrating on his use of language and form, rather than on the metaphysical and social philosophy which is subsidiary in his art.

Cary formed his social philosophy partly on William Blake's views of freedom and creativity, and he drew upon Blake's poetry in order to deepen the characterisation of Gulley Jimson, the artist-hero in *The Horse's Mouth*. Above all, Cary saw Blake's poetry as an example of the kind of achievement towards which he must aim—a comprehensive vision, conveyed by a coherent, vital symbolism. When Mark Schorer wrote what Cary considered to be a faulty review of *Mister Johnson*, Cary explained to him in a letter:

> My novels are all about one world—as much so as
> Blake's poetry is about his world, and I want, like him,

to make people *feel* that world which might be described as that of *freedom*. . . . It includes aesthetic and political freedom, the whole problem of the created symbol. And like others (like Blake again) obsessed with a view of the world which seems to me so obvious, but to other people apparently so dark, I am very anxious to make my world understood and felt. . . . I do not want to start by saying 'this novel is a metaphysical construction based on a comprehensive idea of life' or they will stop entering into my characters' lives and instead treat the book, if they tackle it at all, as a kind of crossword-puzzle, asking what does this character stand for,—or that,—they will imagine an allegory. And I detest allegory—my people are real people in a real world or they are nothing.[1]

Cary believed that novels must contain the specifics of life, yet convey universal insights through the artist's imaginative skill. One of Blake's aphorisms is, 'Spiritual War: Israel deliver'd from Egypt, is Art deliver'd from Nature & Imitation,'[2] and one of his comments on his 'Last Judgement' begins, 'Fable or Allegory are a totally distinct & inferior kind of Poetry. Vision or Imagination is a Representation of what Eternally Exists, Really & Unchangeably.'[3] Cary repeatedly expressed similar beliefs about the art of fiction. In *Art and Reality* (1958) he praised the richness of symbolic realism, in which specific intuitions from life subsume metaphysical truths as well as associations from our cultural tradition. But the parallels in thought and art between Cary and Blake must not be pressed too far. Blake's imaginative eye revolved from the external world to dwell on his own inner vision. Cary's imaginative eye moved from the individual's dreams to the external world where each individual, such as Johnson or Gulley Jimson, tried to find enough freedom in order to fulfil his dream. Cary drew on his own experiences in the external world for some of the dramatic material in his novels.

Joyce Cary was born on December 7 1888 at his mother's family home in Londonderry. His forebears had been landlords in Donegal from 1621 until his grandfather was ruined by indebtedness after the Arrears Act of 1882. Cary's father migrated to London where he trained to be a civil engineer. Subsequently, Cary grew up in south-east and west London; his familiarity with its street life, forms of speech and types of people is especially evident in *The Horse's Mouth* (1944). However, the setting in *Charley Is My Darling* (1940), *The Moonlight* (1946) and his two trilogies is usually Devon, where his family had its origins.

Cary's childhood vacations were spent with relatives in the north of Ireland. He was free from the conflicts which enmeshed his ancestors there, but nevertheless he had access both to a vital family tradition and a dynamic historical scene. *A House of Children* (1941) is an autobiographical novel which he derived from memories of those childhood vacations when he had explored not only his ancestral home, but also his own nature. During those holidays away from the controls of his father and school, Cary first experienced the pleasure and responsibility of complete freedom. For his panoramic view of late Victorian Ireland in *Castle Corner* (1938), he drew on family history, as well as on his childhood observations of customs, dialects, and scenery.

The death of his mother in 1898, and the subsequent death of his kindly stepmother, showed Cary the cruelty of life. However, his relatives, especially at his Great Uncle Tristram's home in west London, were affectionate and understanding towards the young Carys. Many years later Cary wrote, 'We knew, more consciously than other children, what family affection meant, as the one trustworthy thing among so many treacheries.'[4] The traditional values of family love and loyalty are celebrated in some of his fiction, especially *A House of Children* and several stories in *Spring Song* (1960). Cary showed only average scholastic success at Hurstleigh and Clifton. His early experiences at Clifton were unpleasant, and he attempted to run away in his first year after his stepmother died. But he overcame his handicap of bad eyesight, and displayed some prowess at sport and military exercises, which were valued there. He also pursued his interests in story-telling and verse-writing. Otherwise, Clifton had little lasting effect on Cary, except to make him rebel against institutionalised Christianity and academic discipline.

When he was fifteen years old, Cary accompanied a cousin on a sketching and painting trip to France. There he met a broken old academician who, having failed to develop his art, had resorted to imitating his first successful paintings. This meeting supplied Cary with not only an episode for *The Horse's Mouth*, but also a memory which haunted his whole life and drove him to extend continually the range of his fiction. His enthusiasm for the Parisian art world, and an inheritance of £300 per annum from his mother, led him in 1906 to begin art lessons in Paris. An artist-friend, Charles Mackie, advised him to enter the Board of Manufacturers' School of Art in Edinburgh. Cary showed skill in draughtsmanship, but his poor eyesight hindered him and he decided to turn to poetry. However, this period as an art student in Paris and Edinburgh contributed to his representation of the artist's world in *The Horse's Mouth*. The pictorial quality of all his fiction, which is evident in his descriptions of people and places, is also connected with this early training.

After privately publishing *Verses* (1908), an inconsequential collection of his rhyming pieces, Cary entered Oxford to study Law and pursue a literary career. He attempted more verse-writing, and accompanied Middleton Murry, his room-mate, on two expeditions into the Bohemian art world of Paris. But Cary's education at Oxford had little influence on his development as a novelist. He did not do much work except essays for various literary clubs, and he left in 1912 with a fourth-class degree. He promptly took lodgings on the edge of Soho in order to attempt writing a novel about the prostitutes and street life which he and Murry had encountered in Paris. Cary felt that he required extreme experiences as raw material for fiction. Thus, when war broke out between Turkey and the Balkan peoples, he set out to be a stretcher-bearer in Montenegro. His record of the expedition, which was published posthumously as *Memoir of the Bobotes* (1960), indicates that he expected that war to be the last one. The sentimental, dashing side of Cary's personality is evident in his romantic comments about battle and the nobility of peasants.

Through his friendship with Frederick and Heneage Ogilvie, Cary met their sister Gertrude. He fell in love with her almost immediately, but she rejected his advances and her parents doubted his sense of responsibility. It was partly to prove his strength of character that Cary decided to join the Nigerian service as an assistant district officer. In 1916, after his first tour as a civil and military officer, Gertrude Ogilvie accepted his proposal and their marriage took place. They grew to love each other deeply, despite turbulent quarrels. Cary's belief in love as the highest creative value was confirmed by his happy marriage. His wife's encouragement sustained him through the many years before his first published novel, and her practical assistance made possible his large output later. When she was dying in 1949, Cary wrote in his notebook, '. . . the fearful bitterness of this danger to T. [Cary called his wife Trudy] and all our memories together, was mixed with the sense of something that can survive any loss, the power of love.'[5] Cary's intense appreciation of his marriage contributed to his sympathetic grasp of women's viewpoints in novels such as *The Moonlight* (1946) and *A Fearful Joy* (1949). His female characters are not subsidiary or passive, but are as dynamic as his male figures.

Cary had entered the colonial service of Northern Nigeria in 1913. Apart from the desire to prove his character and participate in the romance of imperial rule, he had a political motive. He believed in the stated ideals of Lord Lugard's programme of eliminating oppression and protecting the people in their communal institutions. Cary was first sent to Bauchi Province on the Jos Plateau, where he worked as assistant district officer under various officials who were the sources of several characters in his African novels. The superior whom Cary most admired there was T. F. Carlyle, a 'pagan man' in that he tried to protect his tribe from external influences. Carlyle was the model for Bewsher in *An American Visitor* (1933). When the First World War broke out, the British West African Frontier Force was ordered to conquer the German Cameroons. Cary was eager to enter the war in order to test himself, but he was not interested in the politics of the conflict. At the siege of Mora Mountain, he received a head wound which he at first thought was fatal. These experiences of danger in the bush and tall grass of the Nigeria-Cameroons border were later used by Cary in a few short stories, such as 'Bush River' and 'Umaru'. But the crucial effect of the campaign was to impress on him the quality of the life of the man of action —an awareness on which he based the creation of characters such as Jim Latter in the political trilogy.

When Cary returned to Nigeria from home leave and marriage in 1916, he resumed duties as a military officer at Nafada. He was sent back to the political service in 1917 and placed in charge of Borgu Division in the north-western part of Nigeria. This division was poverty-stricken, undeveloped, and sparsely populated. Cary's first tour there was frustrating because he failed to understand the people. His letters home occasionally burst into tirade, 'But no black man on God's Earth is reliable.'[6] The work of clearing up the heavy backlog of court cases and tax collection exposed him to the worst side of human nature. He was also suffering from asthma and insomnia, but his neurotic outbursts partly showed a failure to engage with reality after his romantic notions about colonial Africa had been dashed.

After home leave at the beginning of 1918 Cary began to understand the Borgawa people's need for the positive components of freedom. He built twelve large bridges in 1918–19, as well as *zungos*, wells, roads and other public works which would widen the possibilities of freedom. He met law-abiding subjects of the empire and he liked them. Tasuki, the detribalised bridge-builder in *Mister Johnson*, was drawn from a man whom Cary knew in Borgu and later praised in *The Case for African Freedom* (1941; rev. 1944): 'He had been flogged by at least one court. Yet he had more brains, guts, and powers of leadership than many of those emirate officials who had taken their pay for fifteen years to neglect the Borgu roads and leave the streams unbridged. Tasuki got his chance of freedom, and seized upon it, not for the pay, but the delight of doing that work for which he had been fitted by nature. . . . For the individual, autarchy, whether primitive or modern, is the enemy of freedom and life. For the state, it is a waste of power, and none, however powerful, can afford to throw away its Tasukis.'[7] In his early days in Nigeria Cary had accepted the prevailing opinion of his peers and deplored 'the loss of the tribal standards and tribal dignity'[8] which was said to result from education and economic development. But in his last months in Borgu, he saw that keeping people bound to the tribe and cut off from the external world was a denial of freedom and creativity. Memories of his years in Nigeria supplied details for his African novels, and affected his view of freedom and political power in later novels.

Cary attempted to write several novels in Nigeria. Despite overwork, heat, humidity, flies, mosquitoes, bad diet, inadequate light in the evening, insomnia, and asthma, he toiled through page after page, only to reject the results as inadequate. He also read a great deal at that time, concluding that Wells and Bennett were at a dead end in their representational fiction, but commenting on James Joyce's *A Portrait of the Artist* (1916), 'Joyce's is a little masterpiece. . . . Joyce aims high and straight, and takes all between.'[9] Joyce's modernist qualities, notably his stream-of-consciousness technique which emphasises his characters' interior reality, later influenced Cary's method of presentation in novels such as *The Horse's Mouth*. Because his wife wanted him to leave Nigeria and his health was failing, he wrote a few formula stories which he sold to *The Saturday Evening Post*. Consequently, he decided that he should retire from Nigeria and divide his time between writing potboilers and serious novels, the former to earn a living and the latter to satisfy his need to create significant art.

In 1920 Cary, his wife, and their two infant sons moved into 12 Parks Road, Oxford, where Cary lived for the rest of his life. He soon found that he was unable both to produce formula pieces for money and to develop his art. The mass-circulation magazines rejected his commercial work when it became more pretentious, and his family fell back on a modest fixed income from inheritances. He had to accept many years of genteel poverty during which he strove with courage and resilience to express his intuitions. He published nothing until 1932, and it was not until *The Horse's Mouth* (1944) was issued that his popular success was sufficient for him to enjoy financial security. During those years before 1932 Cary read extensively in anthropology, theology, philosophy, and political theory, as well as the novels of Tolstoy, Conrad, James, Hardy and others. This reading clarified his metaphysical thinking and occasionally had an explicit effect on his later writing. *The Moonlight* (1946) is an imaginative rebuttal of *The Kreutzer Sonata* (1889). Cary admired Tolstoy's novels, but felt that *The Kreutzer Sonata* misrepresents women.

During the period leading up to the publication of his first novel, *Aissa Saved* (1932), Cary was developing coherent ideas about life, as well as satisfactory aesthetic forms for his intuitive perceptions. He worked over versions of several novels, most of which were set in Africa, but none achieved what he intended.

During the nineteen twenties a few of his activities still reflected the idea of the cavalier-artist which had motivated some of his earlier actions. In 1922 he went to Hungary on an expenses-paid trip which was intended to promote the royalist claim there, but he never had a political interest in that cause. Although he expressed sympathy for the workers during the 1926 General Strike, he volunteered to act as a docker in London. This experience supplied some details for *Not Honour More*, and together with his earlier adventures, probably shaped his presentation of characters such as Jim Latter in the political trilogy (1952–5), and Rackham in *The African Witch* (1936).

But the creator behind Cary's art, and in most of his later personal and public actions, was a moral visionary rather than an adventurer. His developing metaphysical and social philosophy was partly a response to his reading of Blake, Karl Marx and others, in conjunction with reflection on his observations of life in Africa and elsewhere. He also felt the need to formulate an answer to the overriding problems of the day—the advance of totalitarianism in Europe, the futility of prevailing political thought in the depression-ridden democracies and the resultant increase in the number of barriers to human creativity. In his political treatise, *Power in Men* (1939), Cary argued for a new conception of freedom—a positive field of power which is established by education, economic organisation, and social welfare, rather than solely by an absence of restraint. Cary elaborated his theory, with specific application to Africa, in *The Case for African Freedom*. During the nineteen twenties and thirties, he had altered his idea of freedom, parallel with the shift of attitude in some intellectual circles, and made his political thought consistent with his experience of imperial rule. Although Cary had admired some Nigerian colonial officers, in 1941 he condemned the institutions of indirect imperial rule as stultifying, and argued, 'Real freedom then can be greatly increased by social organisation; for instance, by transport which increases a man's power to travel, if he has a taste that way; by education, to put it in his power to learn. . . .'[10] Cary's belief that positive freedom is the paramount political value influenced all his fiction, from the African novels to the Chester Nimmo trilogy.

The British military authorities rejected Cary's attempt to reenlist at the beginning of the Second World War, because he was fifty years old and had poor eyesight. However, he became an air-raid warden, and this involvement supplied a few details for *Charley Is My Darling*. Later he was invited to help prepare a propaganda film on the constructive features of the British imperial system. Although Cary knew nothing about films, he undertook to write the script for *Men of Two Worlds*. During preparations for filming in Tanganyika, he showed his usual sense of humour when, wearing only red underpants and a pith helmet, he came across the governor's formal beach party. Cary walked through the party, tipping his helmet and greeting the ladies and gentlemen as he went. His comic sense was evident throughout his life, and is one of the most pervasive qualities of all his novels.

Cary's behaviour and artistic vision were shaped by his independent faith: 'All we know of God, certainly, is that he is good, that he is love, that he is beauty, that he exists in the world, that is to say, in the universal nature of things as we know it and in ourselves.'[11] Cary's happy relationships with his wife, their four sons, and his friends show the love, honour and loyalty which were the basis of his life. Lord David Cecil, Enid Starkie and some of his other friends have written appreciatively about his goodness and sagacity. The courage that Cary drew from his faith sustained him in the last years of his life, after the death of his wife in 1949 and during the time of his progressive paralysis from lateral sclerosis. He worked on *The Captive and the Free* and *Art and Reality* until a few days before his death in 1957, by employing dictation and a home-made writing machine.

Throughout his career, Cary wrote in a compulsive flow—composing the dialogue and narrative for various episodes, then organising each novel according to the form which his imagination had devised. He believed in the worth and power of art, and his belief is fulfilled by the vitality and insight of his most satisfying novels.

2 Africa and Empire

Aissa Saved (1932) is a partial failure, although it shows the rudiments of Cary's later artistic procedure. In the preface (1952) to this novel, Cary states that he 'cut out' large portions of metaphysical speculation before the novel was first published.[1] But he failed to draw together the remaining pieces coherently and the result is a series of fragmented episodes. He also crowded into two hundred pages about seventy characters, who enact numerous conflicts between Christians, pagans and Moslems. An obvious fault of craftsmanship is his failure to particularise all these characters and events, but the most fundamental defects of the novel are aesthetic and moral.

The central action of *Aissa Saved* is an attempt to end or at least mitigate the effects of a drought: 'the villages were full of half-starved people whose stores were nearly finished, whose children were hungry and who expected to die in the most miserable fashion if the rains did not fall and the crops did not grow.'[2] Cary evokes both the actual drought, and the metaphorical desert of the people's inner lives; the people are limited not only by physical hardship, but by spiritually destructive ignorance and social poverty. The pagan priests, the African leaders of the Christian converts, the Carrs and other figures offer apparently conflicting solutions. But ironically, all their attempts to create a bountiful relationship between man and his world are fundamentally repetitions of only two rituals, which show the similar destructive quality of their responses to the injustice of fate. The imagery of the two rituals—enacting a sexual metaphor of the desired natural event and offering a blood-sacrifice to propitiate divine demands—is also central to D. H. Lawrence's *The Plumed Serpent* (1926).

Cary's treatment of the characters' enactment of the sexual metaphor is much more satisfying than his attempts later in this novel to present the significance of the sacrifices. The priest, Owule, who claims that the goddess of fertility, Oke, needs encouragement, organises the sexual parallel of the fecundity which is needed in agriculture. Cary shows a sympathetic comic sense which conveys both the pathetic and ridiculous features of the affair: 'When she [Yemaja] saw her husband among a group of men she threw her cloth open and danced across the road to a stranger, singing, "In the oil palms, the father is looking for the mother flower, the mother flower is open, she waits for him." But the young husband did not like this joke. . . .'[3] This ritual, which is a simulation of sexual mating, and therefore an appeal for the watering of mother earth with the sperm of the sky god, is presented with humorous realism. But Cary also implies the serious material and spiritual needs of the people.

Aissa is the central character, but it is only in the first part of the book that she is more than a stereotype of African emotionalism. She associates her love for Jesus with her love for Gajere, and her enthusiastic protestantism with her natural sensuality. Unlike the pagans, her linking of sexual experience with religious satisfaction is actual rather than ritualistic. Thus she abandons the proselytising group of Christians in Kolu, rejoins her lover Gajere, dances the Oke ritual, indulges her bodily desires, and spearheads a Christian rain-making crusade against the pagans. After her escape from pagan attempts to have her murdered as a witch, Aissa's first Christian communion is experienced as partially equivalent to a sexual orgasm, 'What would Jesus do inside her? What would he feel like? What would he say? She perceived a faint warmth in her stomach. She brought all her mind upon the place. She held her breath. . . . She found it again deeper and further in. It grew quickly, it was like the morning sun whose rays grow stronger and warmer every minute; it pierced through the cold muscles. . . .'[4] Ironically, this sensual appreciation of Christ's love precipitates Aissa into leading the second Christian crusade on Yanrin and the sacking of various towns.

Cary's treatment of the motif of blood sacrifice begins by humorously revealing Carr's naïveté in preaching to Kolu about Christ's crucifixion and atonement; a local translator incongruously claims that Carr is threatening the people with a vengeful

God who wants more blood before He will end the drought. However, the presentation of the actual blood-sacrifices, which culminate in Mrs. Carr's physical sacrifice of herself and her unborn baby for the missionary cause, lacks moral perspective and psychological penetration. Initially, the fetish priest, Owule, sacrifices Numi and kills this boy's mother, and Aissa later kills Owule, but the drought only becomes more intense. When no rain falls, Aissa and her followers are threatened: 'Every man within ten miles who had spent the morning among his yam hills with his eyes fixed on the sky waiting for the promised tornado, had caught up his spear and run to Ketemfe at the news that the rain-makers were trying to escape without fulfilling their contract.'[5] Cary's grotesque image emphasises the depth of the people's desperation. Although Aissa finds Gajere and Abba in Owule's compound, and tries to retire to amorous pursuits, her fear-ridden followers prevent this backsliding. Aissa's life here reaches its climax. When forced by her followers to make what had been for her a false and unnecessary choice between love for either Christ or her lover and baby, she chooses Jesus. She does not want to sacrifice Abba, whom she loves passionately, but she hysterically denies her own nature and kills her baby over a crude cross. Aissa, who is next sacrificed in this travesty of religious ritual, envisages during the pain of death a reunion with Christ, Gajere and Abba. The religious and sensual are united in her delirium: 'Jesus had taken her, and he was carrying her away in his arms, she was going to heaven at last to Abba and Gajere.'[6] This conventional evangelical image of death contrasts with Aissa's sordid sacrifice and shows the irony of her deception.

Professor Molly Mahood, in *Joyce Cary's Africa* (1964), argues that the title, *Aissa Saved*, is not completely ironic and that Aissa achieves a kind of salvation. This conclusion is faulty because the narrator's tone is cynical, the context of Aissa's sacrifice is sensational and Cary's opinions elsewhere confirm his views about the futility of blood-sacrifices. The narrator describes Aissa's death on an ants' nest, 'She rolled on them, thrashed them with her forearms, crushing them by hundreds. But they were soldier ants born and bred for self-sacrifice. Probably also on account of the bad season they were especially eager to get food for their community. . . .'[7] The cynicism of Cary's attitude towards her sacrifice is evident in this analogy between the action of his characters and the behaviour of the ants. Furthermore, Aissa's last fantasy is induced by hysteria and delirium; it bears no correspondence to any spiritual victory of belief over death. Cary wrote about the novel in a letter to Ernest Benn, 'It [*Aissa Saved*] is however in one sense an attack on one kind of sacrifice. It seeks to show that the idea of sacrifice when removed from that of utility, of service, i.e. pleasing God, pleasing Oke, becomes pure juju and also self-indulgence.'[8] Although Cary's syntax is confused in the second sentence, this summary implies that his title is completely ironic. But this declaration, which states that *Aissa Saved* is partly the vehicle of his opinions, also implies that Cary deliberately neglected art for a moral object lesson. The forces of common sense, as represented by the grotesque figures of District Officer Bradgate and his loyal admirer, Ali, are only marginal to the novel. The blood-sacrifices of Aissa, Mrs Carr, and the others mark the triumph of the destructive over the creative, but Cary's first novel does not adequately dramatise this conflict and its participants.

The improvement in Cary's art between *Aissa Saved* (1932) and *An American Visitor* (1933) is evident in his management of both form and characterisation. His development in narrative skill, particularly in the freer play which he gives to his strengths of comic observation and irony, assist in making a considerable achievement. The ease with which Cary renders the social scene in *An American Visitor*, in contrast with his sensational presentation of religious conflicts in *Aissa Saved*, also shows an increasingly sensitive engagement of his imagination with his material.

The political theme in *An American Visitor* is the dilemma of establishing a creative harmony between freedom and order, and of preventing one or the other from falling into anarchy or tyranny. Cary explores this dilemma in the lives of Marie Hasluck, the American visitor, and 'Monkey' Bewsher, the local district officer. By the time that Cary wrote this novel he was coming to realise that freedom is a dynamic field of power, to be increased by economic revolution and the consequent abandonment of tribal restraints. Bewsher is an ambivalent figure. He has some of the preservationist zeal of the 'pagan man' type of colonial official, in that he refuses to recognise both the historical forces on the side of the tin miners, and the possibility of a larger freedom for the Birri outside their tribal bounds of custom. On the other hand, Bewsher enthusiastically promotes federalism among the Birri, an irrigation scheme, new crops such as onions, a marketing co-operative, public health improvements such as bottle-neck latrines and other practical advances in Birri institutional and material life. His energy thus goes to promoting what he feels to be the only possible conditions for creative freedom.

The Birri themselves fear that the prospectors will requisition their land, and they also hate the previous impingement by the Christian mission on customary institutions and laws. Although the Birri are suspicious of Bewsher's goodwill, he manages to ally himself with Obai, a progressive sub-chief, and to stop the first uprising of the Birri without using military oppression. Cary satirizes the excesses of folly which surround Bewsher, as in this conversation between Gore, his assistant, and Stoker, the military officer, who come to rescue him and the Christian mission:

> He [Stoker] turned to Gore. 'You realise this mission
> is about a mile round. The fool that planned it hadn't
> much idea of how it was going to be defended.'
> Gore fell in at once with this essentially military
> attitude towards the layout of missions. 'And that
> schoolhouse is masked by the chapel group. . . . Don't
> let the missionaries catch anyone in the chapel, I should
> keep out of sight from the mission house as much as
> possible.'
> Stoker gave him a sharp look. 'Don't they know
> I'm here?'
> 'I hope not yet.'[9]

Their military pretensions and discussion of tactics are absurd— the defended do not know that they are being defended, and do not wish to be. Bewsher's goodwill contrasts with Stoker's ridiculous militarism, with the tin prospectors' greed in opening up Lower Nok to mining, and with the Birri's suspicion.

Bewsher is more than a self-deluded administrator who is caught between exploiters and suspicious indigenous people. He is also a tragic leader who tries to establish and preserve a balance between freedom and order which, though impossible in his historical circumstances, is intended to give more scope to human creativity and avoid a destructive hiatus. Bewsher's moral sense and vitality are as manifest in his private as in his public life. He treats both Marie and friends such as the Dobsons with affection and loyalty. When Marie fails to fetch his pistol he gives his life in order to draw off the Birri warriors who would otherwise have killed everyone at the mission station. Bewsher is the first of those creative figures in Cary's fiction, ambivalent as the author is about the man's political position, who responds to his surroundings with that vitality and imagination which are the marks of freedom.

Marie develops from her early Rousseau-esque religion of nature, to the position of Christian pacifism which forces Brewsher to forego his pragmatic method of handling violence. Marie is driven mainly by feeling and sentiment rather than intellect and reason. She enters Birri in the belief that she will find an unspoilt community of peace and brotherhood. Despite being a reporter and amateur anthropologist, she does not observe the Birri accurately: 'These people live in friendship, dignified, self-controlled, contemptuous of the grabber, the buffoon, the envious and the boaster, accepting death like sleep.'[10] Cary humorously shows the irony of Marie's illusion by contrasting it with the Birri's quarrelsomeness. Later she transfers her illusory ideal from the Birri to Bewsher, and tries to summon troops against the Birri in order to defend him. The love between Marie and Bewsher, which humorously but implausibly reaches its consummation in the missionaries' guest-house, shows them claiming the freedom to defy convention and win happiness.

Marie's character alters because of her pregnancy, her spells of fever, her observations of Bewsher's force of character and her conversion to Christian pacifism. Consequently, she refuses to fetch Bewsher's pistol when the Birri make their final attack on the mission. Cary explains that her refusal to fetch the pistol is the effect of temporary religious hysteria, but later Marie states that Bewsher's death had been inevitable: 'And when I couldn't get Monkey safe out of Birri I just had to have Birri safe for Monkey. But I didn't see that if Birri was safe, Monkey wouldn't be Monkey, and if the world was meant to be a safe place there wouldn't be any men like Monkey, and if no one was to die or suffer there wouldn't be any love, and if no one was to get killed there wouldn't be any life worth living.'[11] Cary fails to indicate here the significance of Marie's circular argument, which contradicts her preceding admission of falling for the 'oldest kind of juju'. But her abandonment of the wish to impose escapist desires on Bewsher, although ironically too late to benefit him, shows a degree of self-knowledge which no one achieves in *Aissa Saved*.

The minor European characters in this novel each reflect a single mental obsession, but Cary gives his caricatures a credible basis. Cottee and Jukes, the tin miners, are driven by the profit motive. However, Cottee is imaginative enough to contrast himself with Marie and Bewsher after the latter's death, 'The rest were the cowards, like himself, who were afraid to love, who were afraid of being laughed at; who mutilated and tamed within themselves every wild creature of the spirit. . . .'[12] Although Cottee's observations here, and in his comments about historical change, are shrewd and honest, he is not morally engaged with life. Gore is an eternal civil servant, both afraid to act decisively on his own responsibility, and determined to follow the law and administrative directives to the letter. He is an illuminating foil to Bewsher, who in public life freely disregards all narrow or foolish rules, and in his private relationships lives by creative zest.

A few of the Africans, particularly Obai and Henry, although not central characters in the novel, are individualised more sympathetically than the minor characters in *Aissa Saved*. Cary presents the relationship of Obai and Bewsher with effective dramatic irony; these two imaginative and energetic colleagues in progress are paired in violent death. Cary is not effective in his characterisation of Uli, who breaks a tribal taboo against the frontal position of sexual intercourse; this tribesman's resulting guilt plunges him into contradictory and violent public acts which degenerate into bathos.

An American Visitor has a series of images which help to give the novel cohesion and to deepen its realism by drawing on significant traditional associations. The form of the imagery is at first an actual voyage, followed by occasional metaphorical references to this initial motif. This pattern of imagery is present more comprehensively in works such as Mark Twain's *The Adventures of Huckleberry Finn* (1884) and Conrad's 'Heart of Darkness' (1899). In Cary's novel Marie sets out from 'what we call civilisation'[13] in the hope of finding a natural world of freedom and peace, and her voyage is a metaphor for the interior movement of her mind.

At the beginning of *An American Visitor* Cary describes a chaotic scene of meanness at a Niger River landing. But when the ordinary paddle-boat arrives, Marie feels transcended out of this reality as she gazes 'with an entranced face at the white ship as it floated against the pitch darkness as if in mid-air, with its narrow bulwarks of pearl, its railings and cordage of spider's web, its pillars like ivory needles in the cold unflickering constellation of its own moons; like a piece of another magic world where even machines had grace and dignity. The greasers on a boat like that ought to be seraphim.'[14] The incongruity of her vision is heightened by the description of the riot among Africans for whom there are few places on the boat. A further irony is that the tin miners do have places reserved on this voyage to Marie's Golden Age.

Marie's illusions about Birri are gradually broken, and later in the novel Cary returns to his initial motif in order to convey the quality of her psychological development, as well as to suggest the nature of the imperial system. When Marie, Bewsher and the other men of the civil station are celebrating Bewsher's amazing escape from the Birri at Paré, Marie considers their situation in this extended metaphor:

> The golden age of Greece. Galleys full of agonized rowers bleeding under the whip—chained to battered leaking ships kept from sinking altogether only by the endless patching and plugging of the anxious carpenters creeping about with their tools in the stinking bilges. The lamps flickered in the draught and the waves flowed towards her, she, too, was on a bench listening to the dismal laughter of slaves and there was Gore with a weary dejection nailing up a plank and Bewsher strutting on the captain's plank, shaking his whip at them while they screamed curses. . . . The slaves were chained, the captains, prisoners of the ship. And some day Bewsher would crack

> his whip for the last time. They would throw his old carcase into the sea, Gore would lie drowned among the rats, and she, if she did not die before, would toil on across the black waves—to nowhere—the ship itself, the ship of the whole earth, was rotting under their feet, at last it would open up in space like a burst basket.[15]

This image partly refers to the traditional symbol of the ship of state, and it is qualified by recognition of the basis of Greek civilisation in slavery. Marie had initially referred to Greek civilisation in her earlier illusion of what Birri would hold for her at the destination of the river voyage. The ship here is that of the British Empire, as well as of Marie's mental odyssey. The innocent dreams in her earlier coming have been overturned. This image conveys the impossible political system of apparent grandeur but real oppression in which she sees Bewsher working, and it suggests her own loss of illusions about finding a Golden Age of natural innocence.

In *Aissa Saved* Cary concentrated on African religious behaviour; in *An American Visitor* on the lives of a small group of expatriates. But in *The African Witch* (1936) he attempted to create a panorama of social, political and religious life among Europeans and Africans in a Northern Nigerian emirate under British indirect rule. This novel succeeds throughout the opening chapters in dramatising the complex significance of its political and personal action; however, there is a lack of moral and aesthetic coherence in its middle and final sections.

The African Witch opens at Rimi races, and within the next one hundred pages several more contrasting scenes of riding occur. In Western and other nearby civilisations the horse has been the most powerful form of animal energy which man has mastered. The image of man astride horse has been a traditional means of suggesting an uncertain or dangerous control of powerful forces. However, it is critically faulty to assign emblematic values to horse, man and event in Cary's novel; his mode is symbolic realism rather than allegory.

In *Art and Reality* (1958), Cary analyses D. H. Lawrence's *St. Mawr* (1925) and implies the kind of artistic goal which he had aimed towards in his own novels. Cary's commentary upon the central riding scene of *St. Mawr*, in which the horse shies

before the snake, indicates how Lawrence conveys emotions and
concepts which are beyond yet paradoxically assimilated into
the realistic event:

> . . . their [authors'] greatest triumphs are achieved in
> that narrow space between allegory and the dramatic
> scene. Lawrence's masterpiece, *St. Mawr*, is an
> example. The stallion, St. Mawr, represents the
> uncorrupted male energy, instinctive, free from all
> conceptual whims, entirely real. The scene where it
> throws and nearly kills Rico Carrington is very close
> to allegory. . . . But the intuition was true and
> profound. . . . We are not frustrated by any suspicion
> of allegory. St. Mawr, for all its representative character,
> remains the stallion and Rico Carrington, the poor
> fish, all manner and talk and no real quality of faith,
> of purpose, of feeling, the hollow figment of a man.[16]

Cary is not fully to achieve this kind of artistic goal, which is
illustrated here with reference to *St. Mawr*, until he writes
Mister Johnson, but the initial chapters of *The African Witch* meet
this critical criterion.

In the opening episode at the Rimi horse races, the Europeans
and the Emir's officials are protected inside the enclosure while
the African populace jostle each other outside the ropes. In this
scene Cary presents a microcosm of the British imperial scheme
in Nigeria.

Coker, a mulatto evangelist, and Louis Aladai, an Oxford-
educated claimant to the Rimi emirate, are not part of the
populace or the Emir's officials. The Europeans clamour to have
these two men expelled when they stroll into the enclosure, but
Judy Coote, an Oxford don, engages them in conversation.
While Judy and Aladai retire to talk about local affairs, Rackham
(Assistant Police Commissioner) is engaged in mastering The
Kraken, 'a celebrated sprinter and man-killer.' Rackham resents
the friendliness shown by Judy, his fiancée, to Aladai, and finds
an outlet for his frustrated feelings in the harsh subdual of his
horse: '. . . seeing The Kraken sidling across the paddock, ears
back, eyes rolling to show half the whites, a couple of terrified

grooms hanging to the bridle, he walked up to the brute and gave him a kick in the belly.' The stallion possesses a wild energy, but Rackham overpowers it with brutality. The ride is an ordeal for Rackham; after mastering the vicious stallion, 'he was shaking so much that strangers remarked upon it'.[17] In this episode the action is specific, but it implicitly contains a general comment on the external political situation, the procedure employed to control it, and the enervating effect on the controllers. It also relates to Rackham's later handling of his sexual fears when he thrashes Aladai for having been alone with Dryas Honeywood.

Before the next episode of horsemanship, Aladai's Uncle Makurdi compels him to evade the Emir's ban and enter Rimi in order to guide Judy through Elizabeth's 'juju' house. In the ensuing riot between Aladai's supporters and the followers of Salé, his rival, Aladai finds a horse to quell the disturbance. The narrator states that he 'cantered easily in the open', then that he 'patted it, rested it a moment, and then cantered slowly' in order to disperse the mob efficiently. But when the horse sensed the blood on the ground, 'It reared sideways, with starting white-ringed eyes, and flaring idiot nostrils. . . . Aladai was nearly thrown.'[18] Cary's evocation casts foreboding over Aladai's future. In contrast with Rackham, Aladai at first manages the wild energy of his horse by gentle skill rather than harshness. But, parallel to Aladai's changing character later in the novel, his ride is altered by the effect of the spilt blood.

Initially Aladai, like Cary himself, is a liberal rationalist. In his discussion with Judy, Aladai explains that public education, national institutions rooted in a national consciousness, and technological improvements are needed in Rimi. He also rejects Rimi 'juju' and its religion of blood. Because he realises that political decisions determine the rate and quality of social change, he anticipates becoming Emir. But he overrates his ability both to enlighten the corrupted institutions of the emirate and to influence the inert British colonial regime. Aladai is torn between reason, which Judy represents, and emotionalism, which dominates the personalities of his sister Elizabeth and Coker. Coker's key word is blood, and Elizabeth's career as a fetish priestess is devoted to sacrificing victims for the propitiation of her 'juju'.

Throughout this novel, Cary convincingly shows Elizabeth's irrational powers of invoking autosuggestion, telepathy, hypnosis, and psychogenic illness. He dramatises her mysterious victory in the last episode of the novel; there she punishes Tom, her rebellious kept man, by causing him to retrogress from being a man, to seeming to be a baboon, frog, snake and finally, a 'black jelly, protoplasm'.[19] Aladai's nearness to being thrown by his horse points towards his decline and Elizabeth's ascendancy—the domination of irrationality over reason.

In an early scene which could easily be mistaken for a gratuitous piece of exotic colour, Cary creates a third suggestive contrast in horsemanship—the old Emir riding up to Resident Burwash in order to complain about Aladai's activities. The guards on their wildly rearing horses are followed by the Emir: 'A huge black stallion was now to be seen in the opening, fighting with his bit. He reared at every third pace, catching on his chest the foam that slavered from his mouth. Then suddenly he made half a dozen leaps forward, each of them an attempt to bolt. The rider, a billowing mass of white, out of which a single bird-claw of a hand projected, was seen to sway violently in the saddle.'[20] The significance of this episode emerges in Aladai's revelation that the Emir is tied to his stallion—a puppet swaying in his straps. Thus Cary dramatises the analogy between the Emir's position on his horse and the colonial system of indirect rule. The old Emir's helpless position above the turbulence of his own people is also suggested; later events, in which his Waziri and Master of the Horse organise the usurpation of the emirate and murder him, bear out the implications of this scene.

This series of juxtaposed contrasts continues; in the next episode Musa, the palace rat, and his juvenile gang pretend to be the Emir of Kano in victorious procession. The irony of their mime is sharp. The actors are all liars, thieves and diseased idlers. The satirical humour bites in several directions, as when the narrator concludes, '. . . the last of the gang . . . the stupidest of all, had been given the duty of white men', or when the actors shout in reference to the sore-plagued Musa, 'Make way for the King of the Sudan, blood brother to the King of England.'[21] Musa is a likeable figure, despite his lack of conventional scruples. Although his physique and age are the opposite of Falstaff's, he performs a similar kind of role in burlesquing authority while conveniently attaching himself to it.

The British colonialists unconsciously parody themselves in the game known as Rimi polo. Cary describes their horsemanship on the playing field with ironic humour: trader Honeywood 'was a pretty man in the saddle . . . he very seldom came near the ball'; the Resident's assistant, Fisk, 'had never been in the saddle except in the Banbury Road'; Colour-Sergeant Root 'never hit the ball. Sometimes he hit the ground, sometimes he hit his pony, very often he hit some other player; once he had given himself, by some extraordinary shot, two black eyes'; Rubin's subaltern, Carphew, who boasted of his sporting prowess, 'found an ants' nest in the first two minutes—when his pony fell over it'; Captain Rubin, 'in the attitude of Marlborough at Blenheim teaching the battle where to rage, was bellowing "Get off the ball, damn you! The ball, blast you! Get off the ball—the ball— God damn and blast you!"' and Rackham's pony bit Carphew 'in the bottom'[22] at the climax of the game. This comic affair contrasts aptly with the previous scenes of horsemanship. It is a satirical representation of a sport which is closely associated with British rule in the tropics. The players' approach to the game is unplanned and absurd, just as their treatment of the Africans is unreasonable and inept. Cary here indicates by analogy the intractable relationship of the imperial situation to the colonialists' conventions.

After its remarkable first seven chapters, the novel tends to become diffuse, although events fit the metaphysical structure of the early part of the novel. The conflict between the irrational— in the form of jealousy, fear and hatred—and the rational—in the form of common sense, courtesy and goodwill—is presented increasingly as a series of static tableaux. Instead of creating narration and dialogue which convey the significance dynamically and dramatically, Cary imposes the domination of the irrational as a foregone conclusion. Also, in some of the narration the irrational and retrogressive become only aspects of a distant Africa, rather than part of the Africa which is an imaginative area within ourselves: 'For the difference, even in a snob's imagination, between a peer and a tramp is nothing to that in a savage's between himself and a white man . . . His indifference to the white man and his ideas is founded on a feeling of difference so profound that his mind will not attempt to pass over the gap.'[23] In *The Case for African Freedom*, Cary persuasively disproves this opinion and argues that the change of 'social idea' needed to bring African freedom can be achieved by 'curious minds, found often in the most primitive villages, which desire knowledge for its own sake'.[24] But in the later sections of *The African Witch* he allows common biases to break the bond of sensibility between novelist and reader.

In the central and final parts of the novel, the old Emir's corrupt court is bought by Salé, and the Europeans reject both Aladai's claim to equality with them and his merit as Galadima. The local administrators of the imperial government—Resident Burwash and his A.D.O. Fisk—live in self-imposed isolation from the political facts. The only European in *The African Witch* who has reasonable insight into local politics and customs is the missionary, Dr. Schlemm, but he is rejected by all sides. However, Schlemm is fallible; he wants to employ Aladai's popularity and power for Christianity, and he uses Aladai's infatuation for Dryas in order to lure the young African to his mission. Dryas Honeywood, from a sixth-form sense of social manners, is polite to Aladai, although she feels repugnance towards black-skinned people. Aladai's overwhelming gratitude and affection towards her are unconvincing, given his English public school and Oxford experiences. Cary here falsely endows Dryas with an influence which has disastrous effects on her own life as well as Aladai's. The working out of the metaphysics of the plot demands this blindness in Aladai, but Cary does not create in Dryas the necessary character to make Aladai's insensitivity plausible.

Aladai's self-sacrifice is perverse because, although he speaks of dying for Rimi, he falls into the debased behaviour which he once condemned. When he waits in Dr. Schlemm's burnt-out mission with Osi, his maid-servant, whom he had rescued as an accused witch from Elizabeth, he senses that her fear is an aspect of himself. But instead of trying to revive his reason and understand his fear, he participates in sacrificing Osi to Coker's 'juju' crocodile and embarks on his own death. Cary does not particularise Aladai's final psychological decline into emotionality, but instead falls back on racial stereotyping. Aladai seems to be a hybrid figure. Cary probably combined his later conception of the nationalist as a just leader, with his 'black prince' from an unpublished manuscript of the nineteen twenties; Cary had earlier suspected that nationalists inevitably had neurotic personalities. This would partially explain his inconsistent characterisation of Aladai and the lapse of sensibility in the last sections of the novel, as Professor Mahood has shown in her study.

Cary planned *Castle Corner* (1938) as the first of a chronological trilogy or quartet of novels set between 1880 and 1935 in Ireland, Africa and England. The last event in *Castle Corner* occurs at the time of the Boer War. Cary explained that he did not finish the intended sequels, partly because critics discouraged him by misinterpreting *Castle Corner*, and partly because he did not feel adequate to fulfilling his goal of both creating vital characters and also answering 'universal *political* questions'.[25] In *Castle Corner* Cary sometimes succeeds in achieving his goal, but he often fails because he relies on a series of juxtaposed but depersonalised and platitudinous political debates: the ideas of the ascendancy (landlords, Protestants) versus the aspirations of nationalism (peasants, Roman Catholics) in Ireland; the interests of bourgeois Liberals (High Church adherents, capitalists) versus the polemics of radical Liberals (Chapel members) in England; the expansionism of the empire builders (soldiers, traders) versus the traditionalism of the tribes (Laka, the Emir of Daji) in Africa.

Cary concludes his preface, 'The better I drew my characters, the more they would fail as illustrations of general laws.'[26] This so-called failure is the redeeming quality of *Castle Corner*; by the time he writes *Mister Johnson* Cary has realised that the strength of his artistic procedure lies in the concrete particularisation of characters and their world. In the satisfying parts of *Castle Corner* his representation of characters in relation to their homes and lands conveys political themes by implication. Although the significations of this pattern of imagery derive mainly from the novel itself, and to a lesser extent from our awareness of the social history of architecture, this kind of symbolism has many literary forerunners. A long history of fiction, from *Mansfield Park* (1814), to *Wuthering Heights* (1847), *Dombey and Son* (1848), and *The Spoils of Poynton* (1897), exemplifies the way in which houses signify complex emotional overtones in addition to their specific physical presence.

Cary begins *Castle Corner* by delineating two households which represent the conflict in Ireland. His description, because it touches the particulars of people and places, is far more evocative than historical exposition or political argument could be. Cary knew the Irish scene thoroughly from his family tradition, but he is not personally involved in its turmoil and has an objective point of view. This Irish social scene had been explored by George Moore in *A Drama in Muslin* (1886) and some of his later fiction, but Moore's personal involvement in Irish history gave his presentation a bitter, torn quality, and his method often tended towards moralising rather than objective narration.

Castle Corner in Donegal is the spiritual centre of Cary's novel: 'If one looked to the east, the house seemed to float on the lough, sparkling yellow in the April sunshine; like the yacht of some legendary prince in a sea of Rhine wine. But if one looked out of the west windows into the dark green shadows of the trees and the mountain behind, one seemed to be in a forgotten castle where some sleeping beauty in her country stays might eat hot buttered scones for a thousand years and never hear a sigh, except from the chimney.'[27] This romantic imagery, which associates the house with fairytales, is suggestive of the Corners' attempt to live a fantasy, although history holds another reality for these Protestants in the North of Ireland. Yet the Corners sincerely love their house and land, which are aesthetically satisfying. In contrast with this idyllic scene, on Knockeen mountainside Mother Foy drums the people to her sons' eviction, which has been ordered by their landlord, old John Corner. Con and Padsy Foy prepare to fight the bailiffs and police from their cottage, which they had illegally extended to allow Con to marry Kitty: 'The cottage, lit only by the gleam of the holy lamp, one candle in a bottle and the glow of the fire, was like a cave full of excited gnomes. . . . Each time he [Con] rammed in a sod he uttered a screaming curse against the police or the Corners. Con had sworn to hang for a Corner if they took away his house.'[28] This concrete description implies much about the occupants: religious piety, poverty, violent feelings and a love for their Irish home as sincere as that of the Corners for their house. Cary convincingly shows the complicated feelings of love and hatred which flare up between these two interdependent classes and temporarily stop the eviction, then cause it to proceed later at Old John's secret command.

Cary shows by analogy the Corner family's position in Ireland at the time when John Chass inherits Castle Corner: '. . . the roof was full of rot and the chimney stacks ready to fall. A general reconstruction was necessary.'[29] This comment aptly suggests the religious and social decline of the Protestant Corners. John Chass's absurd but likeable frivolities in his cart race and financial speculations contrast with both the colonising purpose of his Protestant ancestors and the violent nationalist agitation of people such as Con Foy. Cary emphasises the ironic truth of John Chass's position when his only child later dies of tuberculosis contracted from Con Foy's wife. Felix's adolescent son, Cleeve, feels the glory of the Corners' position but he has no sense of reality: 'At Castle Corner, he saw himself the young prince among his people . . .'[30] The mock romance of this passage ironically reveals that Cleeve's sentiments are foolish.

Bridget Foy, unlike the other peasantry, aspires to having the superficially glamorous life which is connected with Cleeve and Castle Corner. She invites Cleeve's sexual advances and bears his illegitimate child gladly, because she thus feels nearer to being rich and aristocratic. However, the truth about the castle for Bridget's social class is shown by Sukey's kitchen in the basement, which is a dark, fiery hole reflecting the latter's personality. Vitality and drink drive Sukey on, but she has no illusions and knows that her place of work is hellish. The behaviour and atmosphere around her reveal the effects of the brutalising labour which maintains the romantic façade of the castle. Ironically, the Irish peasants endure and multiply against adversity, whereas the Corners decline into sterility and decay.

Slatter, a miserly but flamboyant land-grabber, lives in Carnmore: 'Carnmore, built by Slatter on his marriage twenty years before, was a big square barrack, painted butter yellow, with chocolate drip stones. It was like a giant doll's house and everything about it glittered with paint and polish, its brass doorstep, its windows, its new London furniture and gilt frames.'[31] Cary here suggests by analogy the crudeness and ostentation which dominate Slatter's comic character and activities. Slatter openly covets Castle Corner because it represents the aristocratic Anglo-Irish tradition which he, as a Protestant parvenu, would like to obtain. He also wants a son in order to ensure his physical succession, and consequently 'adopts' Philly Feenix, the parson's sensitive son. Slatter's repression of Philip's freedom eventually terminates in the young man's suicide instead of his accession to Slatter's estate.

Cary's descriptions of Felix's African home imply that the senior Corner is not a builder of lasting empires, even if the local situation were more amenable. Unlike his colonising ancestors, who built Castle Corner, Felix settles into the hulk *Maria Fry* and its attachments on the Mosi: 'The station appeared like a deserted ruin, half buried in mud and powdered with the tropical dust of rottenness.'[32] The condition of the hulk corresponds to the sordid moral atmosphere of his trading endeavour. Felix at first rejects the offer of a slave but soon buys her; he rationalises the practical necessity of this act, as he does all his intellectual and moral contradictions. Although he gives garrulous philosophical advice to the young and business tips to his friends, his radical political philosophy and his business sense are laughable shams which reveal one aspect of the decline of the Corners. Cary's presentation of the grotesque figures around Felix in Africa is humorous. Hatto, the glib Cockney trader, Jingler, the African triple spy and minstrel, and the African mistresses with whom the European traders treat themselves are effective caricatures. Harry Jarvis, who is Felix's nephew and the only ambitious member of the Corner family, revives in Africa the imperial heritage which he admires in the tradition of Castle Corner. He repudiates orders and colonial policy, and marches on Daji in order to incorporate it into the Empire. Jarvis is presented heroically, whereas the Emir is a morally depraved autocrat. Jarvis sees his imperial conquest as a civilising task and a chance to bring Britain back to stern duty, but Benskin, the parvenu South African capitalist, uses Jarvis's exploits for mercantile and political advantage.

Benskin's values reside in his money and lands. He wants Castle Corner because it represents for him the first works of an empire-building race. His mammoth red terracotta pile in Devon is suggestive of his outlook and aspirations: 'Its colour was such that the very blue of the sky, the green of the fields, the amber of the trees fading in autumn, the smooth curves and broad planes of the hillside were changed on the eye to the coarse thin appearance of a drop scene. But it was a contemporary master-piece.'[33] Cary's humorous irony is derisory; it is a remarkable feat for a house to belittle the natural scene. Benskin wants an empire that is in the popular modern style of his house—large, materialis-tic and vulgar. Cary fails to particularise Benskin's character as fully as his house is rendered here. He is a passive, grey figure, whose motivation for empire-building is not given an adequate psychological basis.

The clash in England between Chorley's radicals and Benskin's empire-building Liberals lacks substance. Chorley, the main radical Liberal, has no defined quality; his non-conformism is a superficial label. Apart from Porfit, a caricature of Dickensian dimensions, there is no specification of the personal or social motivation on the radical side. This lack of depth and insight is present throughout the English section of the novel. The charac-ters tend to be flat concepts—Mrs. Pynsant representing worldly cynicism, and Cleeve and Cobden standing for pseudo-aestheti-cism. Consequently, the dialogue and conflicts in the English setting show none of the dynamic qualities of life which Cary realises in his Irish and African scenes.

Cary's delineation of homes in relation to characters is at its best similar to what a perceptive representational painter would reveal about characters and places in a series of tableaux. There is some movement and change, such as the decline of Castle Corner, or John Chass's near-bankruptcy, but the pattern is dynamic only through the juxtaposition of scenes. The three geographical areas in *Castle Corner* are connected superficially because each shares some of the main characters with the other two, and all are related to the climax in the construction of the second British Empire. But only the Irish and African sections of the novel are integrated at a deeper level, with the particulars of life convincingly specified in relation to the symbolic centre of Castle Corner. In the English sections of this novel the necessary particularisation and integra-tion of events are lacking. There the narrator's social and political commentary is also more often platitudinous and incoherent than it is elsewhere in the novel.

Mister Johnson (1939) is a major novel of our time. Cary reveals an entire imperial epoch in this work, but he does not employ a panoramic procedure like Conrad uses in order to explore a different imperial situation in *Nostromo* (1904). In *Mister Johnson* the span of time is about one year, the locale is one administrative district in the British colony of Nigeria, and the subject centres on one young African's dreams and relationships. Cary universalises the moral and political revolutions of that time and place through involving the reader in the moment-to-moment enactment of the hero's life, rather than through an omniscient presentation of a large cross-section of distant events. The narration of *Mister Johnson* in the present tense is a rhetorical device for persuading the reader of the immediacy of the times and experiences in the novel. The modernist movement in English literature developed or re-introduced several techniques, such as narration in the present tense, in order to overcome readers' habits of linear response which consecutive linguistic structures and a chronological sense of history provoke. Cary's style also reflects Mister Johnson's imaginative merging of images which are disconnected by time and space. Tropical African cultures, as their traditional plastic arts show, did not displace this unified vision of reality in order to adopt a sequential view of time. Cary's style is thus integral to his content, and a means of closely involving the reader.

Johnson is seventeen years old, buoyant in his emotional excesses, and as neglectful of laws and conventions as Gulley Jimson is in *The Horse's Mouth*. Because Johnson is a southerner in Northern Nigeria, he is cut off from his ethnic roots; his mission school education has given him only a façade of social conventions. He therefore practises the value-free behaviour of a young blade who is not socially restrained by his family and original community. Johnson's freedom from restraint carries with it a solitude which he is always trying to overcome. His exuberant attempts to forge social connections with Africans and Europeans are partial compensations for his alien position. But the crux of Johnson's free life is a dynamic conflict between using vitality for destruction—thefts, debts and eventually murder—or for creation —the Great Fada North Road, dances and songs and affection for other people.

Johnson's buffoonery is a farcical comment on the world around him. A comic event which indicates much about his freedom and the traditional society's rigidity is his engagement to Bamu:

> 'What did we say?' Aliu says. . . . 'So we agreed—six pounds now, and—'
>
> 'No, no, it was five.' Johnson begins to shout. Aliu says something to a dirty little girl, who runs off with the important high step of a hackney. In two minutes, Bamu appears in the compound. She comes in as if by accident. Her brothers look at her watchfully like men selling a horse, and Johnson with shining eyes and parted, greedy lips.
>
> Bamu dawdles slowly across the compound from one side to another, moving each leg only when the other is at rest. Aliu continues to make conversation. . . .
>
> But Johnson can't bear any more. He calls out, 'Bamu, Bamu. Don't you know me?'
>
> Bamu is shocked at this breach of etiquette. She squints sideways at the young man and scowls.
>
> 'Will you marry me, Bamu?'[34]

Cary humorously specifies the villagers' cunning ploys and the contrast in Johnson's honest exuberance. Johnson is here defeated by tribal conventions and cheated out of nearly all his possessions, but he self-deceptively claims a victory. His intentions for a romantic wedding and Christian marriage are made incongruous, both by his own misconceptions and Bamu's traditionalism. But the serious issue is that Bamu and her family reply to Johnson's goodwill with petty treachery. Cary's humorous presentation of Johnson's domestic life is sympathetic; the young clerk loves Bamu intensely, but she returns his affection with disloyalty, and finally, betrayal to the police.

Benjamin, who is sincere, and Ajali, who is fear-ridden, are also aliens from the south. But, unlike their friend, Johnson, they are emotionally inhibited by their loneliness. Cary often reveals their qualities through Johnson's eyes, as in this vigorous appraisal of Ajali's spitefulness: 'You show um a diamond, he tink um broken bottle . . . you bring um beautiful girl, he say she little dirty goat—he creep on his belly all over everyting like house lizard—he say all ting made of dirt.'[35] Johnson's satirical invective, which Cary derived from pithy West African colloquial speech, effectively mocks Ajali's shortcomings. The Waziri is sycophantic, hypocritical, dishonest and wretchedly afraid. Cary makes him a more rounded character than similar figures in the earlier novels, by delineating his personal life—a grotesque homosexual dependence on pretty boys such as Saleh. The measure of Johnson's energetic optimism and ironic self-deception is that, although he is politically powerless, he always claims to have outwitted and defeated the Waziri. Celia Rudbeck is initially a type rather than an individual—the representative traveller to Africa, who uses a condescending language and tone despite a superficial politeness. She is a foil to her husband, who is genuinely engaged with his work in Africa, and to Johnson, who reveals by contrast that her responses are shallow and lifeless. She treats Johnson as if he has walked out of a tale about golliwogs. But Johnson disregards her blasé insensitivity and answers it with goodwill.

Gollup, the Cockney trader, has a violent but curiously equal relationship with Johnson, who is his clerk for a time. Gollup issues insults which range from the label 'nigger' to racialist theories about Africans. But Johnson, through his courage and energy, compels Gollup to recognise him as an individual. They often drink and relate their dreams together. The humorous irony of this dialogue between Gollup and Johnson reveals much about the imperial situation and the meaning of freedom: 'You look at our battle honours, from Talavera to the Somme—there isn't a country in the world where we 'aven't laid down our lives for the Empire, and that's for you, Wog, for freedom—the Empire of the free were the sun of justice never sets. Yess and will again wen they're wanted.'/'I tink some day we English people make freedom for all de worl'—make dem new motor roads, make dem good schools for all people—den all de people learn book, learn to 'gree for each other, make plenty chop.'[36] Although both men are incongruous in their self-deception about imperialism, Johnson's dream of and claim to the British Empire contain much more justice and creative freedom than Gollup's inane boasting. In the brawl that ends their economic and social connection, Gollup's sense of honour prevents him handing Johnson over to the law. Later, at his trial for the murder of

Gollup, Johnson affirms that Gollup was not the object of murderous intent, but his friend.

Although Assistant District Officer Rudbeck is fair-minded, he is at first impatient with Johnson's clerical inefficiency and patronising about his ideas. But once Johnson becomes interested in his employer's pre-occupation with road-building, Rudbeck increasingly becomes the agent of Johnson's creative vision. When Johnson first suggests that they extend the road by using the next annual vote of £150 before it is authorised, Rudbeck is incredulous; despite the inertia of his mind, he eventually responds to Johnson's imaginative ideas. In the final episodes of the novel Johnson again takes imaginative charge of Rudbeck, who feels guilty for having dismissed Johnson. Rudbeck is compelled in law to hang Johnson for murder. But he deliberately commits what is technically also a murder by personally carrying out Johnson's request to be shot. Rudbeck feels 'ever more free in the inspiration which seems already his own idea'[37] after shooting Johnson, whose force of imagination has again moved him out of the rut of rules and conventions. Rudbeck is essentially a passive person whom Johnson inspires to exercise freedom from external restraints—first to help widen their world, then to cut Johnson off from it. Cary shows that the joy and tragedy of freedom are Johnson's.

The traditional tribal culture, the life of the 'new' men such as Johnson, and the British culture of the colonisers are juxtaposed throughout the novel. Cary humorously evokes the tattered quality of the civil station, which is the colonisers' part of the setting: 'The fort, on a slight hill which represents the flattened head-skin of the lion, is a square of earth rampart which has been levelled by time almost to the ground, so that the guard-room just inside it, a mud hut with a porch of corrugated iron, stands up like a miniature cracker hat, a *kepi*, stuck there, on one side of the lion's battered head, in derision. The tin porch is slightly crooked over the gaping door, like a broken peak pulled down over a black, vacant eye.'[38] The lion, which is the popular symbol of the British Empire, is whimsically mocked by disclosing the lethargy and squalor of reality. Cary is not as subtle in describing the traditional community. The narrator, in pointing out that Celia fails to see the truth about Fada, uses overstatement:

'Poverty and ignorance, the absolute government of jealous savages, conservative as only the savage can be, have kept it at the first frontier of civilisation.'[39] Cary is scoring against the traditional institutions and state of mind of the Emir's government, thus revealing the need for the liberation which Johnson and Rudbeck promote with their road. But the tone and vocabulary show a temporary lapse of dramatic subtlety, in comparison with the effectively humorous ridicule of the British civil station. Because political power rests with the imperial administration and the Emir's traditional institutions, the 'new' men have little chance of fulfilling their dreams. Yet Johnson, through his imagination, moves both the imperial administration and the conservative villagers. He appreciates the psychology of both sides enough to take advantage of them if given a partial opportunity. The central irony is that although he appears to live self-indulgently for only the present moment, he actually inspires the building of a road which has revolutionary historical consequences.

A dynamic series of images denotes the construction of this road between two worlds—the oppressive local world of Fada, and the large outer world of trade and new ideas. When Johnson claims, 'De King he say, I want plenty new road everywhere, so my people fit to go walkum, see de worl . . .'[40] he is expressing his need for freedom. Johnson's visionary world of the British king bears little correspondence to the actual outside world. 'De King' is Johnson's metaphor for the liberating power which allows man to 'see de worl'—to experience the larger freedom and awareness which are necessary for creativity. Cary's imagery of the road in this novel is related to the passionate but ambivalent feelings which he experienced during his road-building in Borgu in 1919: '. . . this is as some Roman engineer felt when he strolled down the long reaches of Watling Street, and wondered how long he would be permitted to foretell the future of Britain . . .'[41] Cary had a large estimate of the significance of his own road-building, and this perspective is evident in *Mister Johnson*. He also recognised, as in the remainder of this letter to his wife, that the British Empire would disintegrate—that, in fact, his progressive works would hasten its end.

Like Hardy's description of Egdon Heath at the beginning of

The Return of the Native (1878), Cary's brilliant presentation of the African bush, through which Johnson, Rudbeck and their men push the road, evokes the prevailing atmosphere of *Mister Johnson*. In Johnson's aggressive songs and the narrator's commentary, the imagery of the conflict between men and nature suggests by analogy the modernising and transforming forces in history. Johnson, now foreman, keeps the workers enthusiastically busy by leading them with songs which apostrophise the obstacles to the road:

> *Out of our way, this is the king road.*
> *Where he flies, the great trees fall*
> *The sun and moon are walking on our road.*[42]

This image shows the heroic quality of their work, which is sweeping aside obstacles and metaphorically affecting the cosmos. When funds are finished and there is no alternative but voluntary labour, Johnson levies his own *zungo* tax in order to supply beer and music for the volunteers. Rudbeck does not know about these tactics of Johnson, who spreads his vision of the road among the villagers.

Cary sympathetically but humorously expresses the mythic dimensions of the builders' dreams several times: 'Rudbeck is fond of saying, "When we open this road." Tasuki, Johnson and Audu say to each other, "Ah, when the road is open" in the tone of prophets who look forward to the opening of paradise, to the sound of angels' trumpets.'[43] Until this point in the novel, the road represents the development of trade and communication, the joy of building, and the liberation of an isolated area of the world. But the associations in Cary's image of the first lorry using the road at its completion are ambivalent: 'The little group of hoe-men, their naked bodies glistening with sweat, who stand under these enormous vaults in the hot gloom, are at home. They smile at the road, because they have made it and sung of it, but they have no idea of its beginning or end. . . . Suddenly, in the immense silence of the morning, familiar as the forest twilight, which seems like the very substance of it, they hear a strange noise, between drumming and gunfire.'[44] Drumming suggests both celebration and the threat of war and gunfire is associated with violence. The freedom and expansion which are contained in Johnson's dream of the road are countered by a foreboding of destruction. Shortly afterwards the destructive potential of the road is confirmed by a notable increase in crime. Rudbeck suddenly feels guilty and dismisses Johnson for extortion. The Waziri's henchmen subsequently thrash Johnson for having inspired the revolutionary road-building.

Cary's image of the road—a route opening to a larger world— relates to the romantic history of road and rail developments which opened isolated continents to a wider world in the nineteenth and early twentieth centuries. Whether in the West of North America or the interiors of other continents, the process was destructive as well as creative. Cary's image also has a serious literary tradition in works such as Dickens' *Dombey and Son* (1848). In *Dombey and Son* the railway causes the uprooting and rearrangement of London, and it dramatically kills Carker. Dickens implies the power of the industrial revolution in his particularisation of the effects of the railway, whereas Cary suggests the force of the imperial-mercantile revolution in his imagery of the road. Both authors reveal the complex of good and evil which these historical events hold.

Johnson's dances suggest his love of life, his desire for social ties and his dream of a larger and freer world. He creates spontaneous dances at all his beer parties; he even treats the work of road-building like an expressive dance, keeping the drums and fife playing continuously in order to preserve a creative mood. The imagery of his dancing has literary parallels, such as Yeats's image of the dance of life, but it relates more pertinently to African celebratory rituals which Cary observed in Borgu. Cary also expresses Johnson's imaginative character through songs which are original and striking. Johnson's last song, in which he celebrates the splendour and happiness of life before he is executed, is representative of Cary's poetic ability:

> *Good-bye, my mother sky, stretch your arms all round,*
> *Watch me all time with your eye, never sleep.*
> *Put down you bress when I thirsty; never say give me . . .*
>
> *Good-bye, my night, my lil wife-night,*
> *Hold me in you arms ten tousand time.*[45]

Johnson's songs and much of his pithy dialogue gain vividness and intensity from Cary's skilful use of the West African dialect of English, which has been enriched by images, proverbs and other rhetorical material from local vernacular languages and oral literatures. This last of Johnson's extemporaneous songs evokes the aesthetic and moral grandeur which he sees in life; he reconciles the joys of his past life with the tragedy of approaching death through this vision of an embracing world of love.

Conrad's 'Heart of Darkness' (1899) and 'An Outpost of Progress' (1897), although providing Cary with a precedent for treating Africa seriously in fiction, have a Central African setting and dwell on the European intruder's consciousness. In his African novels Cary attempted to dramatise the people of a culture which was being changed by European impact. Several British writers before Cary set their adventure tales in West Africa, but they were catering mainly to public interest in the exotic and primitive. G. A. Henty's *Through Three Campaigns* (1903) and Edgar Wallace's *Sanders of the River* (1911) were among the most popular of these works which set forth common stereotypes and prejudices about West Africa and its people. Cary's African novels repudiate these debased myths, by moving towards integrity of perception, language and imaginative vision. From his first novel he shows that his knowledge of colonial West Africa, if not complete, is sufficient. However, *Aissa Saved* and the last sections of *The African Witch* are flawed in craftsmanship and sensibility. Although *An American Visitor* is a much less comprehensive attempt to explore African life than the other two early novels, it has moral and aesthetic coherence. But in *Mister Johnson* Cary achieves a comprehensive and significant work of art; there he employs vigorous dialogue and imagery to explore an Africa which is both an historical entity and an area within our consciousness.

3   Youth and Childhood

Charley Is My Darling (1940) is Cary's first novel which presents only English characters in an English setting. Cary's title approximates to a line in a long tradition of songs, from a Jacobite ballad about Bonnie Prince Charlie, to a twentieth-century pop song, but it is probably an ironic reference to Robert Burns's 'Charlie He's My Darling' (1796). In Burns's romantic poem a Highland Charlie came to town, pleased a lass 'on his knee' and upset the whole countryside. When Cary's novel was first published, its realistic subject was topical—Cockney war evacuees in a West Country agricultural community. Several conflicts are implicit in this situation: contrasts between urban patterns of behaviour and the rural setting; clashes between uncontrolled youths and orderly adults; tensions between the forces of imagination and the restraints of convention; and fights between gangs of evacuees. Cary's narration uses mainly the present tense in order to convey the moment-to-moment involvement of Charley in the action. Descriptions are only occasionally given in the past tense, which shifts the narrator's point of view to a more distant contemplation of events. *Charley Is My Darling* superficially resembles the antecedent of many modern novels about juveniles—Twain's *The Adventures of Huckleberry Finn* (1884). But Cary's novel is not extensive in its social insights; its focus remains on the imagination and behaviour of Charley Brown.

Charley's physical qualities are initially important in affecting his relationships and behaviour. He is fifteen years old but undersized. Because he is lousy, his head is shaved and suit burnt. The other evacuees, cruel as unoccupied boys can be, quickly take advantage of Charley's lousiness and shaven head by teasing and physically persecuting him. Consequently, Charley feels compelled to compensate for his humiliations by resorting to boasts and sensational actions. In the preface to this novel

Cary states that young people need help to understand moral complexities. But Charley has little assistance. His stepmother, who is billeted with him, is shallow and foolish. Lina Allchin, the well-intentioned supervisor of evacuees, cannot understand his imaginative needs or personal difficulties. Lina's tolerance unconsciously disguises her hope that young people such as Charley will voluntarily conform to traditional moral and social values.

The opening series of events, which involve Charley's fantasies and experiences with bulls and bullies, define his complex character and indicate the conflicts in and around him. In Western culture the figure of the bull has usually epitomised power and ferocity. Cary's imagery of bulls associates ironically with a long tradition in art and literature, from the frescoes of ancient Crete which show aspects of the Minoan cult of the bull, to Hemingway's preoccupation with the image of the bull in *Death in the Afternoon* (1932) and other writing. In Cary's novel Charley gains the temporary respect of Bill, Ginger and Harry, by boasting of being able to fight Wickens' Devon bull. The bull does not respond to the challenge, much to Charley's relief, but the animal later chases the boys from Wickens' yard. When Charley's shaven head is noticed once again, verbal taunts and violent bullying resume, because the other boys now recognise the incongruity between his attempted dominance and his physical peculiarity. Charley becomes the harassed 'bull' rather than the bullfighter of the earlier episode: 'This kind of human bullfight with a small, angry, desperate boy for the bull is popular everywhere among children. As in real bullfights, it needs only blind courage and fury on the part of the victim and numbers and agility on the part of the players.'[1] Cary's sympathetic irony derives from contrasting Charley's earlier fantasy about bullfighting, with his harsh surroundings in this so-called game.

Cary develops further this sequence of imagery of bulls. Charley, who is hounded by his fellow evacuees and too shamed to show his shaven head at Lina Allchin's class, goes to the abandoned quarry and draws bulls: 'He then makes a blue bull with black eyes set in red circles. He gives it red horns and finally draws curled red strokes like flashes of lightning radiating from it in all directions . . . the bull now looks like a bull of blue fire with transparent horns full of flame.'[2] Charley's desire for the power of the Devon bull is projected into his picture. Above all, in his vivid description of Charley's picture, Cary suggests the angry feelings of this small, bullied youth. When Charley later takes another of his pictures of bulls to Lina Allchin's classroom, she has difficulty in perceiving the animal's shape. She wants conformity and order, which in a drawing means a representational likeness of the subject. The fierce imaginativeness of Charley's picture is as foreign to her as all his imaginative and sometimes illegal behaviour is. To Charley, both the conventions of the adult world and the cruelty of his own generation are antipathetic, so he begins to fulfil his need for recognition and community through crime.

Charley's work in helping to construct Mrs. Allchin's rock garden is the turning point at which he achieves a worthwhile endeavour, but discovers that the conventional world is not interested in creative individuality. From this point onwards in the novel, Charley's imagination is diverted into mainly destructive acts because of the frustration of his need for recognition. Lina and the civil defence authorities wish to build a village air-raid shelter in Mrs. Allchin's front yard, where the old lady had long planned a rock garden. But Charley inspires Mrs. Allchin to rebel and construct on the civil defence authority's excavation what he envisages as a combination rock garden, water-fall, 'real cave', and 'Grand Canyon . . . in Ammurca'.[3] Cary sympathetically but humorously evokes the quality of their relationship: 'The waterfall, by the most careful and elaborate expedients of both artists, working in complete disunity of mind and perfect harmony of taste, is caused to leap from stone to stone as if it had followed its own track for thousands of years. Charley places for it to tumble into a waterworn hollow stone, which Mrs. Allchin removes at least twice a day, and then, compelled by that same masterful taste, puts back in exactly the same position. Charley praises each repetition of his original scheme. . . .'[4] Cary's syntax is here confusing at the beginning of the second sentence, although the passage adequately conveys the comedy of the partnership. The event ends disastrously when Mrs. Allchin catches pneumonia and the authorities seize the completed rock garden for an air-raid shelter. However, Cary treats this episode as if it were a short story rather than an integral part of his novel. Mrs. Allchin does not appear in any earlier or later event. The rock garden episode has a connection with Charley's later compensatory rebellion, but it has no further relevance to other characters and the historical setting.

The repeated motif of Charley's attempt to build a 'cave' suggests his need to escape from unsympathetic adults, as well as from juvenile bullies such as Mort and Bill. The narrator explains the way in which Charley's imaginativeness impels Lizzie and the rest of his gang to transcend their frustrations by going to their secret cave in the old quarry: 'What this means is—the darkness has shut out all Burlswood from us, the bare quarry, the rusty scrub, the broken wire along the lane, and not only Burlswood, but our whole lives in the outside world. . . . Here we are alone in the world and it is a world full of affection and beauty.'[5] Cary's image of Charley's cave is not related to the images of threatening caves in works such as Twain's *Tom Sawyer* (1876). Charley sees his cave as a robber's hoard like Ali Baba's cave, which has associations of romance and adventure. But Charley's cave hut collapses on his gang in a rainstorm. Soon afterwards, as if by analogy, the community comes down upon Charley when his earlier thefts are discovered and the court places him on probation with Lina Allchin.

Throughout the later sections of the novel Charley's fantasies are fulfilled through reckless excursions in the outer world of gang fights and burglaries. The conflicts, in which Charley is cruelly bullied by Mort and Bill, have a thematic connection with contemporary European events leading into the Second World War. The brutality of Mort and his cronies is not a childish game— they nearly drown Charley in the cold pool beneath the bridge. But Charley finally curtails Mort's barbarism, not out of revengeful feeling or righteous indignation, but because Basil had got him to commit himself to a boastful scheme: 'Basil came to him, after midday dinner, armed with two stakes, into one of which he had driven a four-inch nail. He proposed that Charley should hammer this nail into Mort's body. Charley chose the plain stake, partly from chivalry, but also from conservatism. He had used a club before, but not one armed with a nail. "The plain one'll do—you don't want to murder the chap." "Thass wot 'e deserves." "'Ere, got to fight fair.'"[6] Cary incongruously delineates the weapons and Charley's gallantry. The black humour of the presentation is sympathetic to Charley, yet catches the atmosphere of violence in which he is obliged to live.

In his final series of daring burglaries, Charley is not interested so much in stealing goods as in exploring splendid houses and affronting society. As a climax to this perverse realisation of his frustrated desires, Charley holds a burglary party at vacant Burls House, during which he gets drunk and leads the ravaging of its fine pictures and furnishings. While Lizzie hides him from the authorities and they plan their joint escape to 'Ammurca', Charley undergoes a transformation of feeling. Lizzie, who is half-deaf but physically mature, and Charley, who is physically awkward but mentally precocious, fall in love: 'Lizzie has already discovered that the shortest cut to reconciliation is through Charley's desires. But this, to her mind, is perfectly natural and right. She makes no distinction between the physical and the sentimental. . . . Reconciliation was needed because of intimacy, and the effect of intimacy was the need and urge to talk, to confess and to explore themselves. Both tried, with consistent effort, to express something more than needs and passing sensations.'[7] Cary sensitively evokes the verbal tentativeness and physical exploration of their attachment. However, the authorities discover them and Charley is sent for trial.

Charley is condemned for his love, firstly by Lina, his supposed friend, who shames him for getting Lizzie pregnant: 'All his love-making with Lizzie, which an hour before had the beauty of its happiness, now suddenly takes ugly and squalid shapes.'[8] Later in court Charley's feelings rebel against the magistrate's moralistic condemnation of his affair with Lizzie: 'In two minutes Charley is once more in tears. He can't speak. But now, underneath this violent hysterical emotion, there is fury like steel, a deep resolute anger. It is the protest of all his honesty against a lie, and a defilement.'[9] Charley's rage at their condemnatory attitude, which he realises is so severe because of his love for Lizzie, is a moving climax to the novel. He is punished for doing what he knows is beautiful and true, rather than for his thefts and vandalism. Cary effectively contrasts the dishonesty of the punishment handed down by society, with the truth and beauty of Charley Brown's love.

Cary appends an incoherent conclusion to this novel. Charley's escape from a remand home, and the ensuing episodes in which he and Lizzie talk of the possibility of their future marriage, then part from each other in tears, are melodramatic. The nature of their rebellion and love was revealed completely by the scene in court and by the earlier event of Galor beating his daughter Lizzie. The sentimental ending detracts from the truth about these young people's lives, and is a degeneracy into formula.

A House of Children (1941) is an autobiographical novel in which Cary draws on memories of his childhood. The sensations recorded in this book are from holidays with his relatives in Donegal. Cary's preface explains that in this novel facts about people and places are altered in order to achieve imaginative clarity. He also divides himself into two characters—Evelyn Corner, who is the narrator, and a brother Harry, who is two years older. Cary's procedure is unexceptional. Many autobiographical novels, which are based on similar methods, were published in the earlier part of the century; Samuel Butler's *The Way of All Flesh* (1903) and James Joyce's *A Portrait of the Artist* (1916) were two of the most influential. But *A House of Children* is much more concentrated in its time scale and subject than these two novels. Cary recalls in it only his Donegal holidays between approximately his eighth and twelfth birthdays. Although Cary reveals the pain of private frustrations and adjustments in his novel, he shows little concern with the larger Irish social issues which James Joyce treats in *A Portrait of the Artist*. Also, Cary's pleasurable recollections of his family are unlike Butler's bitter criticism of this institution in *The Way of All Flesh,* yet both authors portray middle class, Victorian families.

Cary's stance with regard to himself, his family, the traditional moral framework and Ireland is a result of several factors. His family was understanding and loyal to children, and Cary had a good-humoured temperament. The ordinary strains and monotony of life in his school and his London home were excluded from *A House of Children*, which relates only to his holiday experiences in Ireland. Ireland for him thus became a magic isle, where life could be tested and lived freely. In respect to his lyrical celebration of childhood, Cary's work is similar to Dylan Thomas's more autobiographical *Portrait of the Artist as a Young Dog* (1940).

A House of Children has no plot; its episodes are not ordered to show a dramatic development in the action. Through the first person voice of Evelyn Corner, Cary describes a flow of sensations and events. The work has the kind of coherence which we usually expect in lyric poetry. The 'stories' within Cary's 'lyric' are coincidental to his main artistic intention of describing and exploring his perceptions and sensations about a theme.

The novel opens like the beginning of a long lyric poem:

> The other day, in an inland town, I saw through an
> open window, a branch of fuschia waving stiffly up and
> down in the breeze; and at once I smelt the breeze
> salty, and had a picture of a bright curtain flapping
> inwards and, beyond the curtain, dazzling sunlight on
> miles of crinkling water. I felt, too, expectancy so keen
> that it was like a physical tightening of the nerves;
> the very sense of childhood. I was waiting for a sail,
> probably my first sail into the Atlantic. . . . That
> moment was grasped out of the flux; a piece of life,
> unique and eternal, and the sail also, is still my living
> delight.[10]

As in an extended lyric, Cary introduces immediately the central motif of his work—the sea; he announces the subject—'I'; and he states the method of the lyricist—evoking significant sensations 'out of the flux' of time. This passage is representative of Cary's mode of expression in *A House of Children*; concrete descriptions are interspersed with brief abstract comments. Here and throughout the novel, Cary's attitude is nostalgic and his tone partly elegiac. His evocations of the child's perceptions and sense of expectancy are successful, especially in visual details such as 'crinkling water' and 'squattering into rollers.'

The mystery of the sea was central to Evelyn Corner's experiences in Ireland. His Aunt Hersey's house was on a shelf above the lough. Sea-bathing and sailing were daily rituals in which he felt the danger, challenge and grandeur of life. Cary repeatedly describes the beauty, size and power of the ocean, as in this recollection: 'The house seemed to be full of sea; until, of course, one turned round and saw the real sea so miraculously real in its metal weight and powerful motion, its burning brightness, that it startled. . . . I must have turned myself hundreds of times to catch the sea in its realness.'[11] The sea was thus an accompaniment to the Corner children's happiness, and it dominated their dreams. Evelyn Corner came to feel as if he were a part of the sea; the water suggested to him the elements of change in his life. The Corner cousins sailed daily in their aunt's scow on the often stormy lough: 'The very memory of these roaring days deafens my ears; the continuous howling, like a distant angry crowd, of the wind in our thick shrouds; the groans and shrieks of the sprit against the thick mast, in proportions resembling a carrot . . . and above all, the ceaseless crashing, tearing, boiling, whistling, spitting, sobbing of the broken water through which we smashed our way, makes for the mind a sort of sea tunnel or hollow in the past when one stoops into a long green darkness of excitement and noise.'[12] Cary vividly evokes the intensity of life being tested against nature. He also draws a comparison between the tunnel-like trip on stormy water, and the connection of his childhood with later life. In his sailing, Evelyn Corner concentrated on his immediate present, and was unaware that his future was always streaming into the past. But the mature author nostalgically makes this distinction by commenting metaphorically on his connection with the past, while preserving the immediacy of the child's exciting trip.

Throughout *A House of Children* Cary emphasises the tension of trying to fulfil imaginative desires despite the limitations of inexperience, immaturity and social convention. Some of the most humorous and revealing illustrations of this tension were the younger Corner cousins' plays, which were largely composed by Harry, and produced by themselves. In these plays, the children attempted to transcend life and to live their fantasies. They also intended to gain social esteem as actors by making a favourable impression on their adult relations and neighbours. In their *pièce de résistance*, Evelyn chose the part of admiral; Harry decided to be king, prime minister, and general; and Kathy and Anketel were assigned lesser roles. Aunt Hersey had invited thirty guests to see the production:

But though we had done nothing to avoid disaster,
though we had not even fixed our cues or written down
all our parts, it was not till two minutes before the
curtain that Harry, slowly waving his sword, the sabre,
and repeating his first speech softly to himself with a
look of confident power which would have sat well
upon Napoleon or Marlborough, was suddenly affected
by a doubt. . . . I found myself, for instance, in an
admiral's hat, football shorts and one boot, being
pushed on the stage by Delia or Harry, and hearing
one or both of them repeating words which I faintly
recognised as my part, but which suggested nothing
to me, not even the appropriate use of my only three
gestures. While Delia was saying: 'Your Majesty, I lay
the swords of your enemies at your feet,' I would
feebly wave my sword in the air. . . .[13]

Cary's use of hyperbole and understatement is effective, conveying both the humour of his mature recollections and the pain
felt at the time of the fiasco. The children learnt from this failure
that to realise their dreams is a difficult task.

This tension between imagination and the practical world is
shown particularly in Cary's characterisation of the older cousins,
Frances and Delia. Frances, with her younger cousins' assistance,
treated all her suitors as if they were ridiculous, mooning lovers.
The Corner cousins nearly drowned Mackee, a polite lawyer,
when he was standing on the pier watching them swim one
night. Yet their fantastic self-indulgence was defeated by practical
considerations; Mackee had wealth, a house and social status, so
Frances married him. Delia's life was a chain of imaginative
projects: marrying a rich man, becoming a concert pianist and
being a learned scholar. After these schemes failed she dared to
elope to Scotland with Pinto, an eccentric but artistic ne'er-do-
well who was beneath her social position. Delia triumphed,
because Evelyn's father not only accepted her action, but also
assisted Aunt Hersey in preserving Delia's financial security and
family connections. This compassionate conclusion to Delia's
potentially disastrous stroke of imagination confirmed Evelyn's
belief in the importance of family loyalty and love.

Cary's account has many sharply drawn sketches of other members of the Corner family in Donegal. Aunt Hersey fulfilled the Victorian ideal of womanhood; she was good-humoured, affectionate, dedicated to her family and uninterested in politics or other worldly matters. Evelyn admired his father's wit, vitality, courtly manners and physical courage. Several other figures are sympathetically presented caricatures: Robert, a gullible schoolboy; Uncle James, spindly-legged and crabbed; Pegeen, his kindly housekeeper-mistress; Philip, a cynical, cruel adolescent; Kathy, affectionate but lonely; Anketel, a quietly inquisitive little cousin. Cary, through his narrator, is recalling his own family with affectionate restraint. But his account of some behaviour, such as Philip deliberately gulling Robert into making himself a butt of persecution at school, seems to gloss over meanness and to abandon moral perspective.

A House of Children concludes with the episodes surrounding the community's production of Shakespeare's *The Tempest*. This amateurish production took place in comic circumstances, but the poetry had a profound effect on Evelyn Corner: 'Not only words for feelings, like beauty, love, hate, had taken life and meaning for me; but also concrete substances like mountain, sea, thunder, star, boat, began to have new significances. *Of his bones are coral made.* . . . A tune of lonely spirits, the sober and upright bone with his bass voice and rather austere character at one end, and the glimmering sea treasure, living jewel, rolling its merman's song at the other, in perpetual little curling waves of sound, which fell for ever on the bright sea floor, made of itself the voice of creation.'[14] Shakespeare's images of feelings and things were a revelation to Evelyn, because this play, his first experience of Shakespeare's poetry, touched his sensations of life and nature on the peninsula and sea off Donegal. His imagination here made a significant advance in responding to and appreciating the creative flux of life. But it would be long before Evelyn, assuming his character to be Cary's own boyhood self, would begin to formulate his sensations in memorable literature.

Evelyn in his epic, which he enthusiastically started to write the next day, plagiarised *The Tempest*. However, the grace and vitality of his father's diving won him away from composing his derivative and lifeless epic: 'My epic, as I saw it last, in an old exercise book, when I cleared the attic, stopped in the middle of a line and had drawn over it, in blue chalk pencil, little crude sketches of diving men. Yet the quality of our living experience could be translated only into the experience of poetry which people would not read. They prefer, I suppose, to live it, if they live, in any true sense of the word, real lives: and that is even easier today than it was when we were children.'[15] Cary's syntax and logic here are inadequate. This novel shows by its example that their 'living experience' was susceptible of translation into literature which is readable. His choice between only two options is thus unreasonable, because there is a third and richer option— both to live 'real lives' and to gain greater insight into life through significant literature. Cary's novel is mainly a contribution to this third option, despite the defective syntax and thought of a few passages which intrude into his art with faulty theorising.

Evelyn Corner, who is Cary's *persona*, found Donegal comparable to Prospero's remote island away from the routine of existence. Donegal, like the enchanted island in *The Tempest*, turned out for Evelyn to be life itself. The motif of a protagonist exploring himself in the sea and on a remote shore is occasionally present in literature from *The Odyssey* to W. H. Auden's *The Sea and the Mirror*. At the end of *A House of Children* Cary alluded to this tradition, and implied the artist's responsibility to create anew man's universal experiences. Although *A House of Children* has some imprecision in a few abstract passages, it is mainly an original and coherent novel about Cary's childhood sensations of reconciling his life with the world. *Charley Is My Darling* is marred by a formula ending, but the major part of the novel sympathetically reveals the fantasies and reality of a delinquent youth.

4   The Artist and Society

Cary's first trilogy—*Herself Surprised* (1941), *To Be a Pilgrim* (1942), and *The Horse's Mouth* (1944)—is an innovation in the form of the English novel. English multiple novels had before this been variations of chronicle. The most usual form was a chronological series about a family or individual, such as John Galsworthy's *Forsyte Saga* (1906–21) and Arnold Bennett's *Clayhanger* trilogy (1910–16), told from the viewpoint of an omniscient narrator. The three protagonists of Cary's trilogy respectively narrate their often coincident lives and times from distinct points of view. Cary's contribution to the art of fiction was his shaping of the trilogy as a whole, rather than his presentation of each novel in it. Sara's account, *Herself Surprised,* has the form of an eighteenth-century mock-autobiography. Wilcher's narration in *To Be a Pilgrim* resembles a Victorian memoir in expression, though not in organisation of episodes. *The Horse's Mouth,* which is Jimson's oral account, contains modernist methods such as the stream-of-consciousness technique. The strength of Cary's trilogy derives from his ability to dramatise characters; he imaginatively enters the lives and communication processes of the three protagonists who narrate these novels. The style of each novel reflects its narrator's manner of perception, feeling and thought. By employing this form of trilogy, Cary achieves an illusion of objective truth more persuasively, while maintaining his moral perspective, than he could in a consecutive series or in separate novels. His three novels cohere in a complex pattern of irony, imagery and sequence, which gives aesthetic and moral perspective. He thus reveals the significance of apparently confused matters, such as Sara's homilies, Wilcher's claim to have intended marrying her, or Jimson's violence towards her. Hints in *The Horse's Mouth,* for example, help to show Cary's ironic intention in Sara's homilies.

Herself Surprised belongs to the tradition of Defoe's realistic fiction, which emphasises the details of economic, social, and carnal life. As in its prototype, *Moll Flanders* (1722), the heroine, Sara, is a lively working-class woman. Her carnal desires and economic instincts propel her through a series of unconventional and sometimes illegal actions, which she repeatedly vows to redeem by a return to Christian morality. Like its antecedents, *Herself Surprised* tends to be episodic; the main unifying factor is the involvement of the picaresque heroine in every event. Sara, a domestic cook, is robust, unsophisticated and self-indulgent. From the viewpoint of a jailed thief in the late nineteen thirties, she narrates the story of her life in Devon and south-east England during the late nineteenth and early twentieth centuries. Although she had been indignant with the judge for accusing her of having no 'moral sense' or 'religious principle', she admits her criminality and piously warns, 'So perhaps some who read this book may take warning and ask themselves before it is too late what they really are and why they behave as they do. "Know thyself," the chaplain says, and it is true that I never knew myself till now.'[1] This declaration contrasts ironically with Sara's actions and Jimson's view of her in *The Horse's Mouth*. Cary here implicitly mocks Sara's didactic claims in order to show the hollowness of her moral rules. Throughout Sara's chronological narrative, her true feelings and perceptions, which are expressed in vivid language, conflict with a false religiosity, which is asserted in platitudes.

Sara is a remnant of the newly literate Victorian public. Her stated principles are the spurious sentiments of popular Victorian novels of moral uplift: 'My own daughters laughed at Miss Yonge's books and at me for upholding them, but I told them often and I believe it still that great books should tell of good, noble characters and show them in the real trials and sorrows of life, for God knows there are enough in every life, and everyone of us wants help to face them. I know that Miss Yonge did me much good. . . .'[2] Cary here reveals the cultural source from which Sara draws her moralising pieties, in contradiction to her feelings and vitality. Her favourite reading from among these palliative works is Charlotte M. Yonge, many of whose novels, such as *Pillars of the House* (1873) and others which Sara read, teach Victorian moral proprieties of chastity, resignation and humility.

The tradition of social and economic aspiration to which Sara belongs is reflected in many realistic novels from Defoe's fiction onwards. In succumbing to the sexual advances of middle-aged, middle-class Matthew Monday, Sara is practical and worldly about her needs. The comedy of their marriage derives partly from the incongruity between Matthew's eccentricities and the conventions of his class, and partly from humorous clashes between Sara's brash conduct and that of the middle classes into which she moves. In claiming to be only raising Matthew's status by flirting with and charming Hickson, the millionaire, Sara disguises her own social ambition and sexuality. But Cary occasionally breaks the credibility of his plot for the sake of characterisation, as in the episode of the Sara–Hickson affair at the picnic. In a novel narrated by a wily woman who is careless of facts, Cary might have supposed that far-fetched details would be in character. But narrative logic is broken in the account of Matt leaving her with Hickson at the lake, because Matt's disappearance to Hickson's factory is not plausible. However, Sara's description of the resulting liaison with Hickson reveals her character: '. . . on the water, all sounds are like music and make you feel that joyfulness in the body which would be like dreaming if it was not so lively, and sometimes bad. For every knock was closing the eyes of my soul and opening the thirsty mouths of my flesh. . . . So now in the temple, what with the water and the stillness of everything, even the aspen leaves seemed to be asleep, I did not notice Mr. Hickson or what he was doing, but only felt the joy of the evening, until I came to myself and saw that he was going too far.'[3] The ironic incongruity between sensuality and pious protestation is humorous. In order to gratify her sensual and socio-economic needs with Gulley Jimson and Hickson, Sara destroys her husband Matt and virtually severs relations with her four daughters.

In the succeeding period of Sara's life, Jimson satisfies her vanity and physical appetite, which she tries to conceal by claims of genteel modesty. Cary's control of expression and form is evident in this description of Sara joining Gulley on a Devon beach:

The sun was so bright as a new gas-mantle—you
couldn't look at it even through your eyelashes, and the
sand so bright gold as deep-fried potatoes. The sky was
like washed-out Jap silk and there were just a few little
clouds coming out on it like down feathers out of an
old cushion; the rocks were so warm as new gingerbread
cakes and the sea had a melty thick look, like oven
glass. . . . So it grew sleepy and I forgot myself and he
[Jimson] had his way, yet not in luxury, but kindness,
and God forgive me, it was only when I came to
myself, cooling in the shadow, that I asked what I had
done. Then, indeed, I felt the forebodings of my
misery, and punishment, and I was weighed down all
the evening. But though I jumped out of bed the next
night when he came in to me, I thought it was not
worth while to keep what little decency was left me,
and to deny him what he thought so much of. So I
got back again to him. . . . So it was every night. I even
made it seem welcome to please the man. . . .[4]

Sara's initially honest tone, perceptions and feelings are conveyed
in pithy imagery, which is drawn from her life as a cook and
countrywoman. Her response to Jimson is prepared for by her
sincere physical enjoyment of the beach. She is not consciously
ironic in describing the seduction which follows, because her
beliefs oblige her to express Christian remorse. Cary's internal
control of Sara's narration gives part of the ironic focus, and
The Horse's Mouth confirms Sara's sensuality. Her need to cool
'in the shadow' after sexual intercourse is a comically incongruous
contrast with her pretence of asking what she had just done. Her
statements elsewhere in this novel, which indicate that she is a
head taller and much stronger than Jimson, give this alleged
seduction by him a farcical quality. By the end of the passage she
retires into the conventional clichés of a morality which required
women to deny sexual desire and pleasure. These platitudes are
an unconscious self-satire on the futility of her moral sentiments.
Sara is a woman of intense vitality; she is seldom defeated by
an outworn and repressive code.

Sara's life with Jimson is ended by the re-assertion of her

socio-economic drive. Her material ambition is brought up sharply against Jimson's evident failure in the world, when he beats her for pressing him to hold an exhibition. After Hickson and Sara arrange the exhibition, she finally notices what has made Gulley bitter—the mocking laughter at and the lack of respect for his painting. Later, when she tries to compel Jimson to repair his 'Garden of Eden', which local philistines have damaged, he knocks her senseless and abandons her. Jimson, an embittered artist who rejects 'boorjoy' values and associates himself with Blake's vision, cannot understand a self-made woman who has social aspirations and a sense of economic individualism. In *The Horse's Mouth* Gulley declares that Sara's attempt to make him a worldly success signifies that she has abandoned him spiritually. Yet Sara in *Herself Surprised*, by wanting both Jimson's vitality and some socio-economic security, is true to her desires.

Cary shows that although Sara's egotism clashes with the needs of Monday and Jimson, she sympathises with their shortcomings and admires their good traits. In Sara's life with Wilcher, during which she has to revert to being a cook, she is loyal and compassionate about even the old lawyer's perversions: 'As for those who said Mr. W. was a hypocrite to make so much of church and then run after young girls, I thought of his boils and his hot blood, and I thought, too, of my past deeds.'[5] She is sympathetic to her men's fleshly natures, because she recognises her own character in their lustfulness. Cary employs effective dramatic irony in presenting Sara's assertions of loyalty and class deference to Wilcher, by concealing until the end that she is stealing some of his portable property. After Blanche, Wilcher's covetous niece, has Sara jailed for theft in order to prevent her marrying Wilcher, Sara again resorts to piety: 'A good cook will always find work, even without a character, and can get a new character in twelve months, and better herself, which, God helping me, I shall do, and keep a more watchful eye, next time, on my flesh, now I know it better.'[6] Sara's vitality, which had led her to steal in order to buy paints for Jimson and to educate his boy, is an honest contrast with this screen of Victorian platitudes about controlling her flesh. Despite the restrictions of the law and Victorian religiosity, Sara's innocuous crimes, which occur at the end of her thirteen years of loyal and underpaid service to Wilcher, are morally justifiable and creative.

To Be a Pilgrim (1942) provides a large part of the background of political, social and religious history for the whole trilogy. Cary's allusions to John Bunyan's *Pilgrim's Progress* (1684) indicate the traditional structure of imagery on which this novel is built. Bunyan's famous hymn, from which Cary's title comes, occurs at the conclusion of Valiant's account of his struggles to overcome evil and temptation. Each of the three stanzas of the song has a final declaration of faith similar to the end of this first stanza:

> There's no discouragement,
> Shall make him once relent,
> His first avowed intent,
> To be a pilgrim.

Pilgrim's Progress contains one of the great myths of English culture. Its motif of the pilgrim questing for God is also present in earlier works such as Langland's *Piers Plowman*. In these narratives, the journeys of simple but brave Christians are partly allegorical and partly realistic. The pilgrims confront their own inner temptations and despairs, as well as society's evils and hostility; the former are usually presented in the form of allegorical emblems such as Mr. Malice, and the latter in descriptions of the contemporary world of the author. Bunyan's Vanity Fair is drawn from social conditions in the late seventeenth century. The Christian protagonists traverse these hostile conditions of life, trying to subjugate their temporal existence to God's permanent ideal.

Cary sets out his realistic version of this old myth in order to comment ironically on modern life. The form of Cary's trilogy gives some moral perspective on Wilcher's pilgrimage. However, Wilcher's life-story begins in the eighteen seventies, whereas Sara's connection with him begins in 1926, and Jimson has only slight contact with him. Consequently, the external commentary on Wilcher is not as complete as that on Sara. When Wilcher describes events in his early years, the truth can only be determined through Cary's control of Wilcher's narrative, and through the hints of Wilcher's earlier self in the older self upon which Sara and Jimson comment.

In *To Be a Pilgrim* Wilcher is engaged with the political and religious problems of reconciling freedom with security, revolution with conservatism, spiritual needs with material necessity, moral ideals with worldly temptations, and cultural change with conservation. Cary's overt explication, through Wilcher, of modern moral and intellectual dilemmas is occasionally pointless and banal. But the novel consists mainly of Wilcher's memories of his dynamic personal relations, which only implicitly deal with these dialectical conflicts. Wilcher's consciousness centres on his own generation who are dead—his brother Edward, sister Lucy, brother Bill and sister-in-law Amy. But during his writing, he is also currently engaged with the next generation—his nephew Robert (Lucy's son), his niece Ann (Edward's daughter) and his niece Blanche (daughter of Bill and Amy).

To Be a Pilgrim is intended to be Wilcher's memoir, recorded at the age of 71, during a period of nearly two years after the jailing of Sara. His recollections and meditations occur immediately before the Second World War, but his present serves mainly to provide mental connections with the events of his past. Often a present scene elicits the past; for example, Robert, Ann and Molly rowing a boat recalls by association the Jubilee Party on the same lake. However, memories of past events, such as the deaths of Lucy, Edward, Bill and Amy, sometimes inspire him to consider the meaning of his present life and approaching death. Cary does not present a slice-of-consciousness imitation of the unordered mental processes of a senile old man; he juxtaposes Wilcher's past and present in a dual chronological series and employs an oscillating defensive style which often effectively reflects the old man's perverse personality.

The changes of verb tense in this novel do not consistently distinguish past events from present, though these changes sometimes show the degree of Wilcher's engagement with the episode. The present tense usually indicates greater immediacy of impact on his imagination. Despite Cary's need to sustain the partial senility of Wilcher's character, some of the repetitions detract from the coherence of the novel; for example, Wilcher states many times, in much the same pious clichés, that Sara was a loyal servant and his spiritual salvation. Cary's irony in these instances loses its impact by insistence and becomes monotonous.

Wilcher's character is the basis of *To Be a Pilgrim*. In *Herself Surprised* Sara describes incidents in which Wilcher is an exhibitionist who exposes his sexual organs to young women in London parks; a wealthy miser who pays her badly and allows his houses to deteriorate; a law-breaker who permits his family to use underhanded influences in order to get him off charges of indecent exposure; a disloyal lover who allows relatives to interfere with his private life; and a probable arsonist who burns down his town house during a bout of temporary mental disorder. Sara excuses Wilcher sympathetically by alleging that he is a fine Christian and gentle lover. She explains his meanness by putting it down to excessive material and social responsibilities, and rationalises his lechery by pointing out that he is harmless. Less sympathetic conclusions must be drawn from his actual selfish behaviour to Sara in *Herself Surprised*, and from Jimson's humorous perception of his 'boorjwar' falseness in *The Horse's Mouth*.

In *To Be a Pilgrim*, Wilcher is vividly portrayed as an old man suffering from heart disease and senile disturbance. His mental imbalance and nearness to death give him insights which contrast ironically with the conventional Christian and legalistic formulae of his ideas. After Ann, his doctor-niece, has rushed him from the temptations of London, where he might expose himself to young women or visit Sara in prison, he awakes at Tolbrook Manor, his Devon family seat: 'My veins seemed to rustle with mice, and my brain, like Tolbrook's roof, let in daylight at a thousand crevices.'[7] These similes about his mental condition and bodily sensations are specific, and revealing. The old man's perverse innocence and nostalgia for childhood draw him into the former day-nursery, now a maid's dormitory: 'I said that I had thought to hear voices in the nursery. "Voices", she [Ann] said, and blushed. She always colours when she thinks me strange or mad. She tied up my pyjamas which were falling down, and said: "You mustn't go about like that—I don't mind, but the maids might, and you know we had trouble in town." Ann, whose education is like a set of boxes, all neatly arranged in a filing cabinet, has put me in a box labelled "Exhibitionist".'[8] Cary dramatises Wilcher's compulsive but unconscious behaviour precisely. Wilcher knows that everyone thinks him peculiar, if not mad, but he lapses into these unusual acts as if they were routine activities. He also enjoys the humour of scaring foolish people, especially his agent, Jaffery, who believes Wilcher's partly facetious hint about burning down Tolbrook Manor in order to save his immortal soul.

In *Herself Surprised* Sara mentions the frustrations and loneliness which are partial causes of Wilcher's difficulties. His own account unconsciously confirms that these strains have helped to cause his compensatory gestures for attention. Yet he speaks sarcastically of Ann's educated views, and has refused to allow a psychiatrist to explore the motives for his perverse activities. He explains his own bizarre behaviour as black humour, or as daydreams in which he imagines the dead in their old haunts together, or as mere accidents after which others annoy or scare him by their misinterpretations. But there is also in these actions a crazed and obsessive quality which gives their humour, nostalgia, or spontaneity a pathetic dimension. Cary's irony is complex; Wilcher thinks that he is sane, but others in the novel think him partly demented. In fact, his mental state is much more complex than these labels suggest, and his imagination is potent enough to rebel against the restrictions of confinement and ill health. He always plans to escape and marry Sara, but his first statement in the novel shows, according to events in *Herself Surprised*, that he is deceived about Sara's worldliness and his complicity in her arrest.

Wilcher's memories are often a re-experiencing of the struggle in his life between the spiritual and the worldly. In his references to the eponymous image of the wanderer searching for God, Wilcher regrets the defeat of his spiritual side: 'She [Sara] put down no roots into the ground; she belonged with the spirit; her goods and possessions were all in her own heart and mind, her skill and courage. And is not that the clue to my own failure in life. Possessions have been my curse. I ought to have been a wanderer, too, a free soul.'[9] Wilcher is unconsciously ironic in his excessive self-recrimination and his self-deception about Sara's socio-economic preoccupation. His later memories show that he often had little choice except to preserve his tangible inheritance. His stewardship over the mundane responsibilities of houses, land, money and the legal system also provided a haven to which his brother Edward and sister Lucy could retreat.

Cary specifies both the struggle within Welcher to assert his freedom against the prevailing social order, and the emotional cost for him of the victory of conformity. Wilcher constantly berates himself for not having married Sara but, apart from his sexual aberrations, he was afraid of breaking the bourgeois taboo against marrying one's housekeeper. This conventionality is carried into his old age, as when he condemns the sexual relationship of Robert Brown and Ann, his young custodians. Cary humorously presents Wilcher's hypocrisy, when the old man creeps into Ann's room and catches a glimpse of the couple in bed together, then reprimands her in the morning, '. . . perhaps some of these old conventions about chastity and so on were designed for the happiness and protection of women'.[10] Wilcher's voyeurism and exhibitionism emphasise the hollowness of his cliché about 'the happiness and protection of women'. Cary ridicules the fatuity of a repressive moral and social scheme which has partly resulted in Wilcher's unhappiness and compensatory sexual perversions. The conventional rules won his mind, but not his feelings, and this schism has a pathetic outcome.

One of the crucial tensions in Wilcher's life was political. The public support for reform, even revolutionary action, which he gave his brother Edward, a Radical Liberal, was opposed to the fear-ridden conservatism of his inner life. Wilcher is partly conscious of this contradiction in his character, because he records his political actions with some dismay, 'And I was carried away. I was more ferocious than the dockers. I said of our opponents, "These devils must be fought with their own weapons." And I, too, assured working men in the back streets that all wars were started by millionaires, in order to make money, and destroy democracy.'[11] These words from Wilcher's speech, in relation to his timidity and fear of social change, are humorously ironic. Yet his political behaviour was not deliberately hypocritical. The conflict on the political platforms and in the society of England also took place inside Tom Wilcher, and the conservative self did not win completely in the end.

Edward, like Lucy, broke free from the moral and social order, and both of them died prematurely. Edward was a courageous leader of the Radical cause throughout the Edwardian age—attacking the House of Lords, the industrialists and other powerful interests. He also defied the social and moral codes of that world by neglecting his debts, keeping a beautiful actress as mistress, marrying a rich widow for her money, composing cynical couplets about friends and enemies, and abandoning all family responsibilities to his younger brother, Tom Wilcher. After losing the first election of 1910 by 15 votes, Edward was broken and declined into bitterness. Wilcher's admiration of Lucy's rebellion into spiritual freedom is partly ironic, because her life ended in submission to sectarian flummery, material poverty and marriage to a brutal preacher who committed adultery in her presence. Yet Wilcher concentrates on her passionate Protestant vision, which contributed to the spirit, if not the substance, of England. Wilcher's eldest brother, Bill, and his wife, Amy, accepted the Victorian conventions of a large family, an institutionalised Church and a stable democratic monarchy. They are a foil to the daring freedom of Edward and Lucy, and Wilcher oscillates between the polarities of Bill and Amy on the one hand, and Lucy and Edward on the other.

Wilcher is constantly anguished at the onslaught of cultural change on tradition, especially the English tradition of neo-classical form and order which is symbolised by Tolbrook Manor. When he finds that Robert has converted his Adam brothers' saloon into a storage shed for the thresher and farm tools, he reflects:

> Rakes and hoes were leaning against the classic panelling. . . . Upon the one chair remaining in a corner, a yard cat was suckling two kittens. It needed nothing more to say that barbarians had taken possession. She did not even run from me, but lay watching, with up-twisted neck, and the insolent calm ferocity of some Pict or Jute encamped in a Roman villa. British country gentlemen of the fourth century were, I suppose, often more cultivated than ourselves. Their families had lived for two or three centuries in those beautiful manors, among an art and literature already ancient. . . . And when we look at their bath-houses

> and see the marble steps worn hollow by the naked
> feet of a dozen generations, we feel so close to them
> that we suffer for them in their terror and destruction . . .
> But this room breathes of a double refinement;
> the Roman art of life, distilled through the long spiral of
> English classicism.[12]

This description of Robert's sacrilege, and the analogy between his spoliation and the sacking of the Roman villas in Britain by the barbarians, aptly suggest the destruction in modern life. Cary does not frame Wilcher's emotional words ironically here; at this point Robert seems only a vulgar spoliator. Wilcher's preservationist sensibility has a moral basis. His moving awareness that a high culture was destroyed once before in Britain gives poignancy and strength to his feelings. Tolbrook Manor, like Forster's Howard's End, is an effective symbol for England, or at least for one aspect of English tradition.

Cary concludes the novel with Wilcher's intellectual and emotional realisation that the contraries of life are parts of the creative process in society and individuals. His clandestine pilgrimage to Sara, whom he wrongly thought to represent Christian purity, teaches him the fallacy of seeing life and social change in terms of binary opposites. He recognises that change is both a creative and destructive continuation of tradition: 'It is but a new life which flows through the old house. . . .'[13] Wilcher is referring here to the continuation of his farm, of his family through the re-union of Ann and Robert, who have a baby, and of the established religion which even Ann and Robert acknowledge by attending his family prayers. The focus on the latter event is unclear, because Cary is ambiguous about the motives of Ann and Robert. It is difficult to know whether they attend Wilcher's services in order to humour him and obtain his property, whether they only want to please a lonely old man, or whether they are beginning to accept Christian verities.

Wilcher's last reflection in the novel contains his final realisation of himself:

> I thought I could be an adventurer like Lucy and
> Edward; a missionary. I shouted the pilgrim's cry,

democracy, liberty, and so forth, but I was a pilgrim
only by race. England took me with her on a few stages
of her journey. Because she could not help it. . . . She
is the wandering Dutchman, the pilgrim and scapegoat
of the world. . . . Her lot is that of all courage, all
enterprise; to be hated and abused by the parasite.
But, and this has been one of the exasperating things
in my life, she isn't even aware of this hatred and
jealousy which surrounds her and, in the same moment,
seeks and dreads her ruin. She doesn't notice it because
she looks forward to the road. Because she is free.[14]

Wilcher's mixed metaphor, which identifies England with 'the
wandering Dutchman', is unfelicitous in this serious passage.
However, the conclusion here contains his most complete glimpse
of his own life, and of the victory in it of the preservationist and
conformist. But Wilcher's story shows that his pilgrimage is not
completely explained by this confession of having been a passive
factor in the movements of modern English history. The struggle
within him was never entirely won by the preservationist, tra-
ditionalist, conformist and worldly; he did act with Edward,
despite a terror of the results, in order to alter socio-political
institutions, and he did support Lucy with love during her
evangelical pursuit of God. By helping to conserve the English
legal system, the English church and the cultural tradition in
Tolbrook Manor, he was preserving a social basis from which the
revolutionary and other-worldly could rise in freedom.

The Horse's Mouth (1944) is Gulley Jimson's dictated record of
his life before and at the start of the Second World War. In the
preface to his American *First Trilogy* (1958), Cary indicates that
the phrase 'the horse's mouth', which is race-course idiom for a
'perfect tip', underlines that this third novel is intended to focus
his trilogy—to reveal its final truth while ridiculing the vulgarity
in modern civilisation. Cary uses several methods of narration in
this novel: a modernist stream-of-consciousness technique which
reflects the unordered flow of Jimson's artistic imagination as he
responds to his world and reacts to Blake's vision; comic dialogue
which Gulley employs to gull, fend off, or ironically indulge the
people around him; and some straightforward narrative which

supplies essential facts and connects the other two kinds of expression. The subject—Jimson's consciousness, paintings and society—is more ironically complex than the content of the preceding two novels of the trilogy. In *The Horse's Mouth* Cary's protagonist not only tells his own life, but also projects its essence into large paintings, and compares it continually with Blake's mythic poetry. In addition to contrasting these three levels of Jimson's life in *The Horse's Mouth*, Cary also presents Sara's view of Jimson in *Herself Surprised*.

The Horse's Mouth opens with one of the most satisfying passages in Cary's fiction:

> I was walking by the Thames. Half-past morning on an
> autumn day. Sun in a mist. Like an orange in a fried
> fish shop. All bright below. Low tide, dusty water and
> a crooked bar of straw, chicken-boxes, dirt and oil
> from mud to mud. Like a viper swimming in skim
> milk. The old serpent, symbol of nature and love.
>> Five windows light the caverned man; through one
>> he breathes the air
>> Through one hears music of the spheres; through
>> one can look
> And see small portions of the eternal world.
> Such as Thames mud turned into a bank of nine carat
> gold rough from the fire. They say a chap just out of
> prison runs into the nearest cover; into some dark
> little room, like a rabbit put up by a stoat. The sky
> feels too big for him. But I liked it. I swam in it. I
> couldn't take my eyes off the clouds, the water, the
> mud. And I must have been hopping up and down
> Greenbank Hard for half an hour grinning like a
> gargoyle, until the wind began to get up my trousers
> and down my back, and to bring me to myself, as they
> say. Meaning my liver and lights. And I perceived
> that I hadn't time to waste on pleasure. A man of my
> age has to get on with the job.[15]

The opening stream-of-consciousness images are simple and brief, suggesting the breathless excitement and rapid, hopping movements of Gulley Jimson, the 67-year-old narrator. Then Cary changes to a more conventional style as Jimson recalls the seriousness of his artistic responsibilities. Jimson's impressions reflect the pictorial quality of his artist's imagination. As in *Herself Surprised* and *Mister Johnson*, Cary creates expression which is original and coherent. It has the sharpness of colloquial English speech uncontaminated by popular journalism and best-seller fiction. The vivid images in this opening passage convey several of the central concerns of the novel, such as the impossibility of repressing a free man by institutions. Jimson metaphorically contemplates the rumour that prison will make a man into a fear-ridden animal, but on his release he himself feels exalted by the freedom of the morning. As in the image from Blake's mythic *Europe: A Prophecy*, Jimson's senses extract from the actual world—the Thames, fried fish shops, dirt and oil—the eternal, infinite world of his visionary imagination. To transmute the apparent into the eternal vision of art requires work, so Jimson turns again to his painting.

Cary's theme in *The Horse's Mouth* centres on the conflict between an inhibiting society and the individual artist who requires positive freedom in which to create. Jimson's current work is the 'Fall', which he is painting on canvas in an abandoned Thames boathouse in south-west London. In order to complete this epic, which is to show the forms of man's fall from Paradise into freedom, Jimson needs to overcome poverty, persecution and the difficulties of painting. He tackles these limitations with humour and recklessness because he knows that solemnity and worry aggravate problems. On examining his half-completed painting in the dark, after trying to beg some money from Coker, a tough bar-maid, and menacing Hickson, a rich art patron, Gulley comments, 'A picture left about in the dark will often disappear for three matches, and come back again, at the fourth, a regular masterpiece. Something quite remarkable. But the match went out before I could see whether I was looking at genuine intuition of fundamental and universal experience in plastic forms of classical purity and simplicity, or a piece of bare-faced pornography that ought to be dealt with by the police.'[16] Jimson ridicules both the censorious public and the art criticism establishment in his parodies of their respective jargons. But he is not mocking his own work. In *Herself Surprised* Sara notices his seriousness and sensitivity about his painting, and in *The Horse's Mouth* Jimson pursues his painting of unfashionable Biblical subjects with obsessive self-sacrifice. His humour satirises an anti-pathetic society, and prevents him from being pompous. He knows what his work must aim towards, but he also knows failure. Gulley repeatedly declares that his main practical problem is not materialism or worldliness, but a lack of the material resources and worldly support which he needs to accomplish his creative work. He does not condemn the wealth of the Beeders and Hickson, but mocks the crassness of people who do not respect serious attempts to create art.

Gulley's work is a struggle to realise his intuitions despite the confusion of the conventional and apparent. Cary shows this tension in Jimson's recollections of Sara, who, in one of his earlier phases modelled for pictures which are now in demand:

> Yes, I found out how to get Sara on the canvas. . . .
> The flesh was made word; every day. Till he, that is
> Gulley Jimson, became a bleeding youth. And she,
> that is, Sara, becomes a virgin bright.
>
> And he rends up his manacles
> And binds her down for his delight. . . .
> Materiality, that is, Sara, the old female nature,
> having attempted to button up the prophetic spirit,
> that is to say, Gulley Jimson, in her placket-hole, got
> a bonk on the conk, and was reduced to her proper
> status, as spiritual fodder. . . . I was too busy to enjoy
> myself—even when I was having the old girl, I was
> getting after some ideal composition in my head.[17]

Through projecting himself into Blake's 'The Mental Traveller', Jimson sees his beatings of Sara as assertions of the freedom for creative work. From his viewpoint, Sara's love became sexual possessiveness, but he wanted the eternal female in her for his paintings. His violent behaviour, as Cary indicates in *Herself Surprised*, is brutal and egotistic. Jimson's reference to Sara as 'spiritual fodder' is also cynical. But these words honestly convey his view that the creation of art supersedes the routine world of moral convention and law.

Cary uses Gulley's analogies between 'The Mental Traveller' and the history of art in order to reveal the nature of imaginative renewal. Jimson confesses that his early 'classical' paintings were imitations, but he goes on with his history:

> But one day I happened to see a Manet. . . . And it
> gave me the shock of my life. Like a flash of lightning.
> It skinned my eyes for me, and when I came out I
> was a different man. And I saw the world again, the
> world of colour. By Gee and Jay, I said, I was dead,
> and I didn't know it.
>> From the fire on the hearth
>> A little female babe did spring.
> I felt her jump. But of course the old classic put up a
> fight. It was the Church against Darwin, the old
> Lords against the Radicals.[18]

In his startling image of 'skinned' eyes, Gulley reveals his first creative awakening. By comparing Jimson's inner clashes with external conflicts between revolutionary ideas and established institutions, Cary shows that society and individuals undergo parallel struggles in order to renew worn-out ideas and forms. The use of imagery from the 'mental traveller's' cycle of enslavement and re-creation aptly suggests Jimson's artistic development through styles of impressionism, cubism and other schools. Like Picasso, he finds that each style becomes self-imitative and consequently oppressive to creativity. In a final ironic reference to Blake's imagery of the 'babe', whom Gulley had earlier interpreted as his creative self, he identifies Hitler with the 'frowning Babe' who 'strikes' terror 'through the region wide'. Cary thus implies that the same imaginative energy, which can both renew and destroy old forms, can also be perverted into crazed destruction.

Cary's presentation of Gulley's foray with Coker to Hickson's place for money emphasises that Jimson is a serious artist, whose imaginative vision contrasts with the deceptions which he has used to survive in the world. When Gulley sees his early picture of Sara on Hickson's wall, he is driven by joy to identify himself with Blake's sons of Los. But Coker, like the philistine society from which she draws her values, sees his picture of Sara as ugly and probably pornographic. Jimson then explains, initially with a rare non-ironic candour: "'It means a jug can be a door if you open it. And a work of imagination opens it for you. And then you feel with all the women that ever lived ... drying, dressing, criticising, touching, admiring themselves safe behind locked doors. Nothing there but women's feeling and woman's beauty and critical eye." "I'll admit she might think twice about those legs." "Those are beautiful legs." "Then they ought to have an elephant for Puss in Boots." "Not in a principal boy, you silly, in a picture. Those legs are divine legs, they're ideal legs." "So long as you're pleased with them, old man."'[19] Gulley suggests in terse, concrete phrases the eternal qualities of womanhood which his picture conveys. His diction contrasts with the jargon of the critics whom he often parodies elsewhere. But Coker's norm is a woman's fashion page leg, and she tries to put down Gulley's enthusiasm for the superficially fat leg in his picture as the lewdness of an eccentric old man. Gulley's satiric cut at her conventional notion of a beautiful woman's leg—'a principal boy'—aptly criticises fads in unnatural figures and fashions. Jimson's case attracts sympathy because of the clarity of his explanation about the significance of his picture. This episode is concluded disastrously by Jimson's thefts and a second jail sentence, which destroy Coker's successful negotiation of an income. Jimson has little practical foresight; the actual world has no status for him, except to feed his imagination.

The people around Jimson are brilliantly evoked caricatures, whom he often epitomises in satiric coined words such as 'bio-grubber' and 'boorjoy'. Cary's presentation of their grotesque appearances, actions and speech is plausibly part of Jimson's consciousness of his surroundings. Coker is ugly, belligerent, violent and philistine. Despite her lack of understanding of Jimson's paintings, he sympathises with her when she is rejected by the community for having an illegitimate baby. Hickson, the millionaire whom Sara charmed in *Herself Surprised* when he had vigour, is seen ambivalently by Jimson as a mean, fear-ridden old 'boorjoy' who deserves to be blackmailed, as well as the only appreciative patron he ever had. By effectively caricaturing the language and motives of Professor Alabaster, Cary ridicules the pomposity and silliness of much art criticism. His portrayals of Sir William and Lady Beeder satirise the ignorance and gullibility of wealthy collectors who never purchase a picture until it has received the imprimatur of a critic such as Alabaster. Gulley's trickery, in looting their flat and later selling them his own forgery of a picture from his earlier phase, is thus ironically justified. Nosy is an awkward, intelligent schoolboy: his idealism in seeing art as pure beauty and truth is the butt of Jimson's exasperated but humorous raillery. Cary's treatment of Plant, who is Jimson's old friend, and the other amateur philosophers of the artisans' education group contains no personal mockery; his ridicule is directed at their far-fetched beliefs in Spinoza and other ideological cults.

Almost all of these subsidiary figures have memorably comic actions and dialogue which are generalised enough to satirise widespread follies, but are specific enough to show the individuality of each person. Only in his characterisation of Ikey, the junk dealer, and Abel, the sculptor, does Cary's satire lose its originality and moral perspective. His ethnic stereotyping of Ikey is flat, and the humour of the dialogue in which Gulley tries to bargain with him is limited by Gulley's involuted games with pounds, shillings and pence. Cary seems to have aimed at satirising Abel's Bohemian pretence to being an artist. But Abel's dialogue is too exaggerated, as in this account of his model-wife: 'She once nursed a block of Portland for me, through ten degrees of frost, in the middle of Salisbury Plain, when a lorry broke down. Put her own clothes on it. Saved it. And caught a pretty severe chill too. Luckily only on the inside.'[20] Humour has to have a semblance of possibility, but Abel's statement has none. Rather than ridiculing Abel's vulgarity, the presentation seems to be cruelly nonsensical.

Cary is concerned throughout this novel with the relationship between art and life—with the connection between the imagination creating its intuitions in painting, and striving for its desires in life. In an episode at a Sussex resort, after enjoying the inspiriting natural scene, Jimson reveals this tension which dominates his life. He imaginatively attempts, as in Blake's *Marriage of*

Heaven and Hell, to reconcile the visible fallen world with the eternal 'world of delight'. Jimson's flaw, which is evident in this and many other actions, is a moral and practical failure to detect that the freedom of the imagination which is needed in order to illuminate these contraries through art must be curtailed in life:

> I put two cards in each envelope and stuck them up.
> A door to glory. The larks had stopped singing. Coming
> down, I supposed. . . . Yes, I thought, fixing my
> eye on a superior pub. The angels must always be
> surprised when some man dives head-first into dirt,
> and then just by a twist of his imagination comes out
> again as clean as a comet with two wings bigger than
> the biggest in all heaven. I had my eye on the saloon
> bar, and just then a young man came out. Nice young
> man in a blue suit, with a dark blue hat, and new
> shoes. But green silk socks. So I drew up level with
> him and let my arm touch his and all at once I showed
> him an envelope and gave him the wink and said,
> 'Want any postcards, mister? Beauties of Brighton.
> Nice new view. For artists only. Plain envelope.'[21]

Ironically, Gulley's cards are decent views of the local sights, which he sells for a large profit. In an outcome which is similar to many of Gulley's attempts to exercise imaginative freedom in life, he meets disaster when a racketeer beats him up for invading the local pornography market. In his paradoxical image of the larks 'coming down', Gulley implies that visionary power is increased by experiences in life; he sees himself emerging from the dirt 'with two wings bigger than the biggest in heaven'. In *Herself Surprised* and this novel, Gulley's earlier paintings of Sara depended on his intense experience with the subject. His action in cheating prurient tourists who want to buy pornographic postcards also has an inverted moral justification. Nevertheless, when Jimson kills Sara at the end of the novel, Cary shows the moral limitations of Jimson treating life as if it were all 'fodder' for his artist's imagination.

The conflict between creativity in a free imagination, and destruction in a blind, changing world, is emphasised in the last episodes of the novel. Gulley finds a derelict chapel and hires a gang of art students to assist him in painting his colossal 'Creation'. He defeats neighbours' complaints of obscenity, an official delegation's attempt to have him paint a general's portrait and the Council's warnings to leave the premises. In the end the Council destroyed his wall around him, and thus obliterated his painting of the 'Creation'. This ironic event, which results in a broken blood vessel for Jimson, seems pessimistic, although he remains determined to create his vision and laugh at destruction. Cary succeeds here and throughout the novel in giving a convincing representation of Jimson's character and world.

Some reviewers and academic critics[22] condemned Cary's first trilogy for lacking moral and aesthetic focus. However, Cary's control of expression within each novel, and of content and form over the entire trilogy, achieves a complex but coherent work. Wilcher appears to Jimson to be a 'boorjoy' philistine, and to Sara to be a Christian gentleman who has slipped slightly in the control of his sexual nature. In the total perspective of this trilogy Wilcher's conscience-stricken, warped and semi-demented personality is a manifestation of the moral and socio-political conflicts of the Edwardian and inter-war years. Despite his disturbed emotionality and moral hypocrisy, his conformist life as a landowner and lawyer helped to maintain a social and cultural basis, however imperfect, from which free, imaginative rebels, such as his sister Lucy, brother Edward and, by implication, Gulley Jimson, could pursue their visions. In *The Horse's Mouth* Jimson often feels that Sara is a possessive female who uses her sexual appetite to consume men, while Wilcher in his memoir initially praises her Christian piety and sacrificial class deference. In *Herself Surprised* Cary not only presents the tension between these appearances which the two men notice; he reveals that beneath this surface of personality is Sara's essential moral quality of feminine vitality, which is based on honest responses to her emotional desires, and which Jimson catches in his paintings of her. In *The Horse's Mouth* Cary shows that Jimson's virtue lies in his creative work—the pictures, which by implication are as imaginatively penetrating and vigorous as his verbal apprehension of reality and his response to Blake's poetry. Jimson's flaw is his failure to notice and accept that human relations require moral curbs on freedom. Cary's satire is not directed against Jimson's work; only his follies and those of people and institutions in his surroundings are ridiculed. No direct authorial comment could better suggest Jimson's genius than giving him a brilliant poetic expression, and associating him coherently, but independently, with William Blake, the greatest English poet-painter.

Cary's focus in his trilogy centres on the motif of the quest for the apocalypse. His allusions to the two great English versions of this quest—Bunyan's *Pilgrim's Progress* and Blake's mythic cycle of poetry—provide an emphatic but integral symbolic framework for his trilogy. The themes of Gulley Jimson's pictures also provide an overt set of references to this motif. Jimson, Wilcher and Sara have some correspondence with figures in Blake's apocalyptic vision—Los (creativity), Urizon (conformist reason), and the Eternal Female. Cary's ironic use of this pattern of imagery is based on the contrast between his realistic fictional mode, and the mythical modes of Bunyan and Blake. The latter authors projected their ideal visions into their art, whereas Cary's realism presents fallible but vital men and women trying but failing to fulfil their visions.

To Be a Pilgrim has some infelicity of presentation, but *Herself Surprised* and *The Horse's Mouth* are satisfying novels. Cary's quotations from Blake's poetry, which are a referential map to Jimson's imaginative processes, show by the comparable strength of the surrounding prose that Cary's achievement is a major one. His versatility and range in this trilogy are wide—modernist methods of using imagery to help achieve moral and aesthetic coherence, traditional modes of humorous dialogue and caricature for satirical and ironic purposes, and techniques as varied as stream-of-consciousness narration and mock-autobiography for conveying the different characters' grasps of life. Cary integrates these many elements and achieves an original and entertaining revelation of twentieth-century life.

5   Women and Social Change

In Cary's earlier novels, women such as Sara are often among the main characters. However, in *The Moonlight* (1946), and to a lesser extent in *A Fearful Joy* (1949), Cary attempts to create a woman-centred world which, as in the parallel case of his African novels, not only deals with that world continuously, but also breaks free of literary conventions which are related to restrictive cultural and social conventions. Several novelists, such as Jane Austen, D. H. Lawrence and Henry James, have created rounded women characters. But female characters in English fiction are often elaborated from traditional stock figures; the sex-objects in fabliaux and the figures of innocence in romances are two of the most familiar prototypes. It often does not matter that female characters are nebulous romantic figures or other conventional types, if, as in many of Conrad's novels, women are peripheral to the action. However, *The Moonlight* is fundamentally about the lives of women.

Cary's preface (1952) to *The Moonlight* (1946) contains several uninformed notions about the history of female emancipation and dress fashions. Nevertheless Cary stresses that the main source of this novel was his 'violent reaction against *The Kreutzer Sonata* [Tolstoy, 1889] which seemed so ludicrously wrong-headed about the whole matter of sex.'[1] Ella, the chief character in *The Moonlight*, believes that passion, marriage and child-bearing are necessary creative goals for women, whereas Pózdnyshev, the protagonist of *The Kreutzer Sonata*, argues that passion is the beginning of debauchery, and that marriage is an enslavement to debauchery. Tolstoy's novel is a formally perfect construction for conveying the emotion of misogyny, which often stems from man's disgust with his own desires. In his novel Cary attempts to overturn the ideas and attitudes implicit in Tolstoy's novel, and to dramatise women from their viewpoint as potential childbearers.

Tolstoy and Cary emphasised events involving performances of two of Beethoven's compositions—the Sonata in A Major, Op. 47 ('Kreutzer', 1803) for piano and violin, and the Sonata in C-Sharp Minor, Op. 27, No. 2 ('Moonlight', 1801) for piano—in order to focus the themes of their respective novels. Tolstoy's Pózdnyshev perversely declares that Beethoven's 'Kreutzer Sonata', as played by his wife and her probable lover, hypnotised him into seeing their illicit relationship innocently; he argues bitterly that this sonata was really a sign of his wife's adulterous debauchery. Cary's Ella, on the other hand, sees the 'Moonlight Sonata' as a musical image of romantic love and womanhood. Ella's vision relates to Beethoven's inspiration for this sonata; he founded it on Seume's poem, 'Die Beterin', in which a maiden prays at the high altar, and he later dedicated it to Giulietta Guicciardi, whom he probably loved at the time of composing the sonata.

Cary's novel is based partly on the dramatic irony of initially withholding from the readers, and from Amanda, who is a principal character, the fact that she is the offspring of Aunt Ella's adulterous love affair. The action proceeds in two interconnected chronological sequences: a period between spring and autumn of one year in the late nineteen thirties, during which the changes of seasons emphasise the psychological movement of Ella and Amanda, the central characters; and a much longer period, between the early eighteen seventies and late nineteen thirties, which exists in Ella's memory and is elicited from her by stimuli during the year of the main action. In her flashbacks, Ella oscillates between assertions of personal freedom, and sympathetic understanding of others such as Rose; her ambivalence is both an integral part of her character, and Cary's technical device for presenting the truth about past events and people. However, the larger part of the novel is presented in the third person by an omniscient narrator. Cary uses the agricultural cycle of the West Country scene—from lambing to haying, fair-going, sheep-dipping and harvest—as a suggestive analogy for the creativity which Ella and Amanda are individually trying to foster and understand.

The opening chapters introduce the central themes and characters, and are representative of Cary's narrative method in *The Moonlight*. Aunt Ella Venn, 72 years old, is trying to arrange a

marriage between Amanda, 32, and Harry Dawbarn, 28, while
Aunt Rose from her sick-bed tries to thwart Ella's plan. After
sending Amanda and Harry into the garden at evening, Ella
plays the 'Moonlight Sonata'. Amanda is coldly intellectual and
the music holds no passion for her. Harry's physical advances
arouse her lust and consequent self-revulsion. To Harry, human
sexuality is a practical and even humorous matter, almost an
integral part of the agricultural cycle which he lives as a farmer's
son. Neither of these two accepts the romantic notions about love
and womanhood which Ella associates with the 'Moonlight
Sonata': '. . . emotions of tenderness, excited by thoughts of
Amanda, were mixed with sensations of exaltations, sacrifice,
danger, mortality and pride, all that belongs, in the minds of old
ladies like Ella, to a woman's fate as bride, wife and mother; a
confused and cloudy world of large vague impressions which in
a modern brain could have been instantly brought down to
very commonplace physical events, no more than enough to fill
out half an hour's gossip at elevenses.'[2] Cary's irony in the last
clause, which satirises the trivial practicality of twentieth-century
life, suggests by contrast that Ella's 'confused' Victorian vision of
love and motherhood is as substantial as more recent values. Cary
draws sympathy to Ella's feelings by contrasting them with the
emptiness of the modern gossips' talk about 'commonplace physical events'.

Nevertheless, Cary is critical of Victorian moral and social
values. He often frames Ella's memories satirically, as when
Amanda queries her about Grandfather Venn, whom Rose had
prevented from dying in his mistress's bed: '"She [Rose] took
you to kidnap him away from Mrs. Wilmot. . . . But do tell me
about Mrs. Wilmot—what did she look like? How old was she?
Did she have any babies by Grandpapa?" "Darling, please—and
by Grandpapa. As if he were—a horse . . . he was breathing when
we carried him downstairs. But I could not be sure that he was
quite breathing when we took him out of the carriage. He seemed
so cold, and, oh dear, his mouth had come open. But we took
him to bed and put hot bottles round him and the doctor wrote it
down in his certificate that he died at the Villa."'[3] Cary's black
humour stems from the incongruity between Amanda's impatience
with Victorian hypocrisy, and Ella's genteel insistence on the

moral discretion of carrying Venn home to be certified dead in his own bed. Ella's naïve exposition of that macabre action lacks any understanding of the related causes of her own unhappiness. Rose had harshly applied the same rules of respectability and duty to Ella.

Through Ella's flashbacks to the Victorian lives of herself, Rose and Bessie, Cary specifies the tortuous conflicts between and within them. In response to the dilemma of reconciling natural desires with cultural order, Rose suppressed her own emotional needs in order to maintain the Venn family as a respectable institution after their mother died. Bessie's will and cunning enabled her to use the institutions of marriage and motherhood as a camouflage for indulging her desire to have a large family and several lovers. But Ella was neither self-disciplined nor cunning; her belief in the institutional values of marriage and motherhood was as sincere as her natural passions. Ella's resultant personality was at odds with itself; for example, she stated that she wanted to keep her lover, Ernest Cranage, but added that Rose was correct in separating her from him and their baby, Amanda. Her compulsive contradictions are still evident in her old age, when she loses Rose's new will: 'She . . . balanced the envelope upon the top of the hot tank. She thought, "It's under my eye there, but gracious! it's not really a good place. Suppose it slipped."'[4] Only through this wilful self-deception about losing the will can Ella reconcile her loyalty to Rose with her determination to buy Harry a farm and see Amanda married to him. Cary here reveals the distorting pressures of Ella's past by narrating this event as if he were within her mind.

Amanda is outwardly reasonable, both in condemning the deficient moral order of the previous generation, and in discussing modern life. However, when she discovers that she feels sexual desire for Harry and her married cousin-lawyer Robin, and that Ella is her mother, she is filled with nearly hysterical sensations: '. . . the grey headless Mary Jane in the corner with its absurd tortured waist, its forced-out chest and stomach, became the characteristic form of that for which it stood as representative Victorian woman, a sensual victim and machine, a fleshly device for the production and nourishment of other little lumps of flesh. . . . But the sight of her own white and plump leg thrust into the moonlight startled her into a new horror—of herself.'[5] The hyper-bolic image of the Victorian dressmaker's dummy in Florence Villa suggests how that age distorted sex into a tempting but for-bidden mystery. Cary's overdrawn description shows the gross-ness and self-alienation in Amanda's recognition of her own suppressed sexuality. She is unable to assimilate her disturbing feelings into her reason.

Cary's presentation of the fair is central to the novel; he des-cribes this vestigial form of the rural midsummer rite of ancient England with clarity and intensity. It is partly a sexual ritual in which the girls become intoxicated through dancing, cider and fairground rides. Despite Amanda's accurate appraisal of the anti-rational component of this event, she succumbs to the emotional atmosphere and allows Harry to make love to her: 'She saw Harry's cap against the sky, he had not troubled to take it off. She reflected, "Isn't he even going to kiss me first—but no, he isn't very religious. Or, perhaps, it's because—he is so reli-gious, yes mediaeval—they used to dance and juggle in church."'[6] Cary tersely conveys Harry's abruptness and Amanda's puzzled acquiescence in the act. For the country girl the fair should preface marriage and motherhood. But Amanda's participation is incongruous—she is 32, educated, and decidedly unprepared for Harry's yeoman salute, which is comically unromantic. She is only momentarily overwhelmed by the strange power of this traditional rural reconciliation of nature and culture. Cary shows that this event is as irrelevant to her modern state of freedom as Rose's middle-class Victorian code is.

Amanda asserts her freedom and refuses to marry Harry, although she is pregnant and Ella buys them Quarry Farm. Amanda's reluctance is partly because Harry casually postpones the date and has another woman, but more because she is unable to conform to a traditional marriage. Cary shows Amanda's assertion of freedom sympathetically, but he implies that her generation lacks the feeling and vitality which Ella possesses. Robin, the young married lawyer with whom Amanda plans an affair, gushes idle opinions without any feeling. This death of emotion is stressed at the end of the novel when Amanda meets Robin accidentally in London: 'He suddenly took her in his arms and they kissed. It was, however, only an experiment.'

Cary implicitly criticises modern life in his ironic reference to 'experiment', but he recognises that Amanda has a freedom and consequent self-sufficiency which Ella never had. Later, Amanda 'lifted her hands and put them on her waist. She was growing big. She said to herself, "But do miracles happen? It will be interesting to see."'[7] Cary thus concludes the novel with a restrained promise of new life in the following spring, although the banality of Amanda's speech detracts from the emotional coherence of his conclusion and shows a slackening of narrative control. Cary's control of facts in this novel also has a few lapses, such as Amanda referring to old Venn as her uncle instead of her grandfather.[8]

The auction of the Venn family property, the preparation for which begins after Rose's suicide, and the completion of which occurs at the time of Ella's suicide, is a metaphor for the destruction of values and institutions which constituted high Victorian culture. Ella's suicide, is a final, though apparently unintentional act of remorse, because she suffered from the delusion of having caused Rose's death. Earlier in the evening she had played the 'Moonlight Sonata' to Amanda and her remaining relatives: 'And it seemed to her that the whole age of Bessie and Rose and her own youth, of love expecting sacrifice, even seeking it, of moonlight walks, of passionate dreams which contemplated nature itself as the grave and splendid cathedral of ideal devotion, had gone for ever. She alone, in that room, had the faintest notion of it. Only she knew that it was not in fact sentimental, but violent, bitter, tragic.'[9] The narrator's commentary here, which moves from irony to pathos, is a sympathetic summation of Ella's life. She is one of Cary's most plausible heroines: her torn sensibility is expressed throughout with aptness and vigour. Ella's ideal of love, which she had so tragically tried to achieve, is associated with the central image of the novel—the 'moonlight', which is the name of her favourite sonata and also refers to the night-time occasions when Amanda recognises the force of sexual desire. The moon is often personified as a woman in myth and literature; Darwin noticed that it has always been thought to have a mysterious connection with the physiological cycle of women; and moonlight is traditionally the atmosphere of romantic love in literary works such as Keats's 'The Eve of St. Agnes'.

Cary effectively integrates his characterisation and action with this and other suggestive images, such as those pertaining to the agricultural and seasonal cycle, and to the dispersal of the Venn family possessions.

A Fearful Joy (1949) is a chronological account of events in the life of Tabitha, a medical practitioner's daughter, between about 1890 and 1948 in London, South-East England and the Midlands. This novel seems partly to take up the intention that Cary dropped when he decided not to complete the sequels to *Castle Corner*. He states in his preface (1952) to *A Fearful Joy*, 'I would try to lay bare historical change not just as a surface, but in its roots.'[10] But in *A Fearful Joy*, as in *Castle Corner*, Cary fails to achieve a penetrating and coherent novel which 'lays bare' the lives of people in history. His narration of historical events sometimes contains the banalities of the popular press and political speeches.

A few of the central figures, especially Sturge, the art patron, are inadequately characterised. Not only are many historical scenes similar to scenes in Cary's previous novels, but several of the narrator's comments, such as those on the evacuees in Chapter 114, are repetitions from *Charley Is My Darling*, the first trilogy, *The Moonlight*, or *Castle Corner*. Although the character of Tabitha supplies a focus for the novel, a few episodes, such as Tabitha's holiday with her brother's wife in the middle of her 'aesthetic' period, are superfluous appendages.

Tabitha lives for the immediate excitement of each moment, but the novel covers a long span of history from the last years of Victoria to Attlee's Labour government after the Second World War. Cary's use of present-tense narration is not coherent with this broad historical scene, which requires some distancing in order to sustain an illusion of authoritativeness. The almost continuous use of the present tense in *A Fearful Joy*, combined with a lack of coherent arrangement, also tends to give the novel a hurried and disorganised quality.

The strength of *A Fearful Joy* lies in Cary's characterisation of Tabitha and Bonser; the historical setting only becomes vital when they occupy it together. The opening section of the novel, in which Tabitha rebels against Victorian respectability and runs away with Dick Bonser, has pace and vigour. Because Tabitha's brother and sister-in-law, who are her guardians, righteously condemn Bonser for being dishonest, lazy, debt-ridden, and foppish—the antithesis of the ideal Victorian gentleman—she finds him free and exciting. Although she recognises the deception of his stories about vast inheritances, noble blood and passionate love for her, she makes the spontaneous decision that determines her life: 'Yes, it must be love; I'm *fearfully* in love.'[11] Cary takes his title from Thomas Gray's 'Ode on a Distant Prospect of Eton College' (1747). Gray's scenes of youthful joys, which have a background of mutability, aptly relate to the paradox of Tabitha's repeated but brief engagements with joy. Although she becomes aware that her feelings for Bonser are preposterous and dangerous, she enjoys her moments of intense happiness with him. Cary humorously delineates Bonser's comic rascality, as when he and Tabitha run off to Bloomsbury: 'Bonser has found only a temporary post in a partnership with a friend. The two have co-operated in a bullion deal, the sale of a gold block to a farmer who, knowing something of economics, has a deep distrust of banks. This transaction has yielded a large profit.'[12] Bonser's bilking of the farmer, and the farmer's gullibility, are satirically understated, as if the deal is a standard transaction between an ethical enterprise and a wise customer. But even in presenting Bonser, one of the most effective pieces of characterisation in this novel, Cary sometimes repeats his previous works, '"My guts are made of tripe; my liver and lights are real cat's meat; I've got egg in my egg; my bottom doesn't hang on a gas bracket; I don't wear my face to hide my back hair."'[13] Bonser is gloating over swindling some bookies, and is impressing young Tabitha with his verbal dexterity. But some of these incongruously funny phrases are employed by Gulley Jimson in *The Horse's Mouth*.

In the second section of *A Fearful Joy*, Tabitha becomes Sturge's mistress and thus creates security for her son, John. Sturge is a wealthy art patron during the last stage of aestheticism—the 'fin-de-siècle' period of Ernest Dowson, Oscar Wilde, and other 'decadents', whose pretensions Cary satirises. In *The Horse's Mouth* Gulley Jimson effectively mocks the values of this period of art, but the repetitive scenes about bogus aesthetes in *Castle Corner* and *A Fearful Joy* lack specification and wit. This part of

A Fearful Joy also contains some superficial authorial commentary, such as this passage on the moral and social changes at the
turn of the century: 'For a duke, the poorest of his rank, is still
a moral power, which sets limits to the freedom even of princes,
so that they naturally prefer for hosts, new men, climbers who
utterly depend on their good will. And this will is for distraction.
It is boredom that has broken the immense fortress of the old
Christian society.'[14] This allegation is not adequately specified
in the events of Cary's novel, and in the light of historical facts
about the alteration of the 'old Christian society' of England,
his conclusion is facile.

Cary's characterisation in this section of the novel lacks pre-
cision, except in the presentation of Tabitha's maternal obsession
with making her son John into a traditional gentleman. She
revels in the exciting, nihilistic milieu of debauched artists and
writers, but she is determined to keep John away from them, to
give him Christian values, and to send him to good schools. Her
unconscious hypocrisy is continuous; she always enjoys a free,
rebellious life herself, but tries unsuccessfully to make her descen-
dants into conformist gentle-people. The artists in Sturge's coterie
are stereotypes: Manklow, a political satirist who is more cynical
and corrupt than most of the people whom he satirises; Boole, an
alcoholic, debauched poet who never finishes a work; and Professor Griller, who has no critical values, but only an eye for
fashion. These stock figures would have more significance if
Sturge, the personage with whom they are all connected closely,
were specifically characterised.

The third phase of Tabitha's history begins after Sturge's
death in the Edwardian period when, disgusted at her brother
Harry for refusing to pay for John's education, she marries old
Sir James Gollan. Gollan is a self-made capitalist and technological innovator during the last stage of the British Industrial
Revolution. To the extent that Gollan is a more convincingly
vital character than Sturge is, Cary illuminates this aspect of
history more adequately than he does the previous one of aestheticism. The creative drive with which Gollan re-shapes material
civilisation is shown by his enthusiasm in developing machines
such as the aeroplane and moving bench. Cary fails to show coherently the character of John, who reaches physical maturity

under Gollan's financial care. At each stage in the novel John seems a different figure—a spoilt brat, intellectually confident undergraduate, London playboy and sheepish university don—rather than a developing person.

In the last section of the novel Tabitha tries to overcome her solitude and bitterness by re-joining Bonser during the historical degeneration before and during the Second World War. Bonser's character is partly a metaphor for this aspect of British history, as Gollan's and Sturge's were for earlier periods. Bonser lives parasitically on the economy at large, as well as on the material and emotional resources of individuals such as Tabitha. He only repays her with the sensations of excitement and freedom which come from companionship with a dashing, imaginative rascal. In the London brothel where Tabitha loyally goes to tend Bonser when he is dying, his deathbed monologue is significant of both his character and historical epoch: '"They thought—Dicky Bonser, he's a gentleman—fair game—honourable family—got to put up with anything. But they didn't think of this one—Dicky diddled 'em—as a gentleman—gelmanly—and didn't care a blast—for anybody—because you see—he *was* a gentleman—good family—". And his eyes close again, he murmurs something about his imperial ancestors.'[15] Ironically, in his dying patter Bonser claims to have practised fair play and gentlemanly honour, two celebrated values of English culture which he has always violated. Bonser's reference to imperial ancestors also suggests his connection with recent British history; Cary's description of his sordid death is thus partially a satiric metaphor for the end of an imperial tradition.

Tabitha's character is based on the conflict between her desires and her conventional ideas of social worth. Even towards the end of her life, after John's death, she tries to make Nancy, her promiscuous grand-daughter, into the kind of respectable wife and mother which she has never been herself. In the last paragraph of the novel, Cary describes a bout of sharp pain in Tabitha's chest, and sums up her life: 'Gradually the pain becomes less, the terror falls away before the longing, the prayer. She perceives that she is not going to die that afternoon. And as, cautiously straightening her back, she looks again at the sky, the trees, the noisy quarrelling children, at a world remade, she gives a long deep sigh of gratitude, of happiness.'[16] Cary here suggests the cunning vitality of an old woman who has always tried to create joy, despite the confusion and hypocrisy of her thought and moral code. In relation to her engagement with modern English history, and in contrast with her sole descendant's abandonment of her for New Zealand, Tabitha is here analogical to England itself— a 'world remade'.

The partial artistic failure of *A Fearful Joy* is not caused by inadequate characterisation of Tabitha as a woman, but by faulty craftsmanship in the presentation of the historical setting and of several male figures. In *The Moonlight* the expression is generally fresh, and the form is coherent with the material. Cary compels sympathy for the viewpoints of Ella, Amanda, Rose and Bessie, whose lives variously reveal the conflicts between personal needs and social constraints. This novel successfully conveys the significance of historical changes in the rôles of women, by specifying individual people and places convincingly.

6   Politics and the Individual

Cary's political trilogy—*Prisoner of Grace* (1952), *Except the Lord* (1953) and *Not Honour More* (1955)—spans the history of England between the eighteen sixties and the aftermath of the 1926 General Strike. Cary had previously failed in his chronicles, *Castle Corner* (1938) and *A Fearful Joy* (1949), to transmute the public and private life of modern British history into art. Since Henry James's *The Princess Casamassima* (1886), many of the important British novels with political themes—for example, Joseph Conrad's *The Secret Agent* (1907), Aldous Huxley's *Brave New World* (1932) and George Orwell's *Nineteen Eighty-Four* (1949) —have dealt with emotional and ideological extremes. In their political fiction, which is often in the form of fables accentuating their thematic message, Conrad, Huxley and Orwell projected tendencies which threatened European civilisation, but which were more marginal in British political life. Cary recognised the dangers of oppression and violence in modern politics. However, his political trilogy concentrates more on central British political experiences. Although Cary does not draw a close documentary connection between, for example, his characterisation of Chester Nimmo and the life of Lloyd George, the realism of this trilogy is parallel with actual political history. The novels in Cary's second trilogy are again narrated respectively by the three main characters, though their lives are more inter-linked than the main characters are in the first trilogy. Cary extends his form of trilogy by experimenting with new techniques in order to convey Nina's qualifying memory in *Prisoner of Grace,* and to suggest the police-woman's transcription of Jim Latter's oral report in *Not Honour More.*

Prisoner of Grace treats the complete political scene, which Cary saw as consisting of relations in the public affairs of government and in the private institution of marriage. In this novel Nina narrates the story of her relationship with Chester Nimmo, a successful Radical Liberal politician. The historical setting covers the last phase of British national expansion, from the conquest of the Boers, to the socio-economic reforms of successive Edwardian governments, the victory in the First World War, and the surge of prosperity in the mid-nineteen twenties. Part of the action takes place around the imaginary Devon port of Tarbiton, which is Nimmo's constituency, and part takes place in London, where Nimmo has set up a home during his successful career as a Liberal M.P., and eventually, as a cabinet minister.

Cary explains defensively in his preface to this novel that Nina is seriously intended to be a prisoner of Chester's grace, rather than merely a fear-ridden liar and egotist, and that the bracketed second thoughts in the text indicate her awareness of other people's points of view. Cary here touches on two aspects of an important problem for the modern novelist and his reader: how to maintain an illusion of objective and complete truth, while implying moral values and determining the reader's sympathy for those values. In Cary's first trilogy, *Herself Surprised* modifies *The Horse's Mouth*, and moreover, Jimson's account of himself in the latter novel is qualified and enlarged internally by descriptions of his Biblical paintings and references to Blake's mythic poetry. These implicit commentaries help to give a complex but coherent view of the truth about Jimson and his world of art. But the mock Victorian memoir by Chester Nimmo, the central character in the political trilogy, does not contain several levels of internal ironic contrast between its protagonist's life and his imaginative vision. Consequently, Cary originated the device of Nina's bracketed qualifications and second thoughts in order to let her reveal more of the complexity of Chester Nimmo and his world of politics. The bracketed expressions often felicitously show the emotional and moral dilemmas of Nina and Chester Nimmo, as well as reflect the workings of Nina's mind. But the parenthetical insertions are sometimes irrelevant and repetitive, rather than indicative of Cary's moral perspective. The constant doubling back and qualifying also result in monotony and slowness of pace. Variations of intensity, which are necessary to indicate the relative importance of events and moral questions, are lacking.

Nina returns occasionally in her memory to experiences with

Jim Latter on the Longwater and the sea. These images of sea trips provide a fragmentary analogical commentary on the characters and themes of this novel. Nina's first reference to this motif—Jim Latter and herself as naked children challenging each other to risk their lives in stormy water—aptly foreshadows their passionate but violent adult relationship. But unlike similar motifs in *A House of Children* and *An American Visitor*, the imagery of Nina's sea memories in *Prisoner of Grace* is not always integrated with the action and characterisation.

At one point Nina uses a vivid extended metaphor, which is drawn from her recollection of a nearly fatal childhood sailing escapade with Jim Latter. Jim had kept up her morale, in order to maintain her needed assistance, by pretending that he had always planned to sail through the bar at Callacombe. Only after their miraculous landing in the storm did he admit his foolishness and fear. Nina explains Chester Nimmo's character and political tactics by making this analogy between his life-long behaviour, and Jim's boyhood pretence that the Callacombe sail had been reasonable: 'And no one has any right to call Chester, who had ten times more imagination than Jim, a hypocrite for pretending in the middle of a political storm (which went on all his life; he was never "in harbour"—there is no such thing in politics) that he had always meant this or that when, in fact, he had only taken note of it as a "way out". The truth is that a man like Chester, just because he had such a lot of imagination, such power of putting himself in other people's places and minds, was *nearly always sincere*.'[1] Although Nina's illustration is consistent with her recurring image of the sea as a metaphor for life, the use of brackets and italics is strained. Cary attempts to connect her childhood sailing experience with Nimmo's constant political need to contradict his earlier policies and enact major deceptions. But comparing the children's physical self-preservation with Nimmo's political self-preservation inadvertently leads to moral incongruity rather than insight into Nimmo's motives and principles.

Nina claims that her memoir, *Prisoner of Grace*, is intended to forestall the forthcoming 'revelations', which she thinks will be based on gossip and half-truths; she anticipates a book co-written by her daughter Sally and Nimmo's ex-secretary Bootham, a history by an Oxford woman, a memoir by Aunt Latter, and other reports. The structure of the plot consists of a series of expected accusations against Nina and Chester, interspersed by Nina's lengthy refutations. Nina's rebuttals of hearsay, for example, that she was 'trapped into marriage'[2] with Nimmo, or that Nimmo was a 'crooked'[3] politician, are complex. Her anecdotes and explanations often confirm and complicate, as well as refute the expected allegations. Together with Nimmo's memoir in *Except the Lord* and Latter's report to the police in *Not Honour More*, Nina's refutations show the tensions of grace and egotism, love and lust, honesty and deception, rhetoric and truth, freedom and bondage, and creativity and destruction within and between Chester Nimmo, Nina and Jim Latter. But in *Prisoner of Grace* the narrative of accusations and rebuttals is often static, because Cary imposes this conceptual framework at the expense of concrete specification of character and politics.

Cary concentrates this trilogy on Chester Nimmo, a lay preacher and political radical who rose from the rank of labourer to become a cabinet minister. The conflict between honesty and deception, as well as between creativity and destruction, are centred in his character. Nina asserts that when she first met Nimmo he had been an ambitious but socially gauche politician; however, he saved Aunt Latter from a scandal, while gaining himself £5,000 and social prestige, by marrying Nina after Jim Latter, her cousin, had left her pregnant. Nimmo carried Nina off into marriage with courteous formality, not forgetting a marriage-bed prayer, 'I had been a little startled on our first night together to hear him murmur (but we were both so nervous at the time that I was not sure if I had heard him properly or if he knew what he was saying) something like a prayer for God's blessing on our union. . . .'[4] Cary ironically contrasts Nimmo's religious ideals with the fact of Nina's pregnancy by Latter. Creative deception was Nimmo's method of overcoming the moral and political contradictions in his life. Although he was often comical, his obsessive belief in an ideal Christian world provided him with rhetoric, and occasionally, moral substance, for his marriage and political career. Whenever he or Nina fell short of his Christian code, he pretended successfully, as here, that they were still following God's scheme, thus creating dignity and self-respect where there might otherwise have been shame and mutual recrimination. It is not surprising that Nina eventually saw Chester as an agent of grace; he carried her from certain scandal to the centre of British power. She is taken from Jim Latter's love, which is tinged with hate, to Nimmo's grace, which, paradoxically, is tainted by and created in deception.

Nina's respective ties of 'grace' and 'love' to Chester and Jim reflect her attempt at reconciling ambivalent needs. Her first realisation that Chester's deceptions were not entirely destructive, but often creative of harmony in marriage and democracy, occurred when she recognised her guilt in attempting to leave him the first time. Her conflict of needs emerged when she and Latter made love in Nimmo's garden:

> But now I must confess something, because it has real importance—I mean, not so much in my life as in Chester's, that Jim, on this occasion, and for the first in my life (I had no idea even of the possibility of such a proceeding) did certain things which at first only surprised me and shocked me a little, but afterwards gave me a most extraordinary experience. So that I seemed (and was) quite lost in it, and said to myself (which was quite wrong, because, as Jim confessed to me long afterwards, when we were really intimate, he had picked up the idea in India where young people actually learn it out of textbooks), 'It is because we love each other.'[5]

The first parenthetical clause is awkward and partially redundant, but the next two bracketed comments ironically disclose Nina's later awareness of having been deceived into believing sexual virtuosity was the same as love. The incongruity between her illusion about love, and the actuality of Jim's Indian artifice, is humorous, and emphasises the similarity between herself and Chester, whom she claims was even more deceived by her later 'Indian' attentions to him. Yet she did love Jim, while feeling the greater force of Chester's moral intensity. Nimmo used his rhetorical skill to make her feel guilty when she tried to run away to Jim afterwards. She argued that he was tricking her about the value of forgiveness and 'duty' in their marriage, which he claimed had been 'so fruitful in results—in our work together'.[6] But she believed that his moral superiority outweighed his petty trickery, and that the role of their marriage in his egalitarian political cause made her sexual need for Jim seem mean and selfish. Although Nina concludes that Chester's moral imposition was an undeserved favour, this episode is partly ironic, as is Cary's title for the novel. Nimmo's dynamism was motivated not only by moral ideals about society and marriage, but also by egotistical ambition and lust.

Cary's representation of the conflict between truth and deception in Chester's political life is neither as profound nor as convincing as his insights into this tension in the personal lives of Chester and Nina. Nina begins her defence of Nimmo's involvement in a major political scandal, the Contract Case, by asserting that it was as innocent an affair as the Marconi Case, an actual scandal which nearly ruined Lloyd George's career in 1913. Nina's parallel is not a convincing vindication of Nimmo, because the Marconi case was inexcusable. In the Contract Case the facts show that Nimmo had deliberately bought shares in a company which was about to benefit from a government contract. However, Cary intrudes into Nina's narration with a plea resembling that part of his prefatory essay which explains Nimmo as a 'man of principle', and condemns critics who interpreted this political 'manager' as a 'crook': '. . . the truth was (and is) that Chester *did not have information*. He did not do anything that any clever business man would not have done, and won great praise. But owing to the very special conditions of politics, and the way people treat politicians, looking for a chance to find the smallest fault with them, and quite ready to invent faults that don't exist, it would have been *quite misleading* for Chester to have told the whole story of Banks Rams. It might have produced a *great injustice,* that is, the ruin of Chester's career.'[7] This defence of Nimmo's character lacks intellectual and moral penetration into his motives. Like Nina's defence of his other political actions, such as his giving up his belief in land nationalisation and becoming a capitalist, her explanation is incongruous and does not indicate anything except her self-deception. Cary's explanation, in the preface to the novel, of his intention to reveal the moral basis of Nimmo's political compromises shows that the control of presentation in this episode is unsatisfactory. The portrayal of Chester's betrayal of pacifism, in return for the post of Minister of Production in the War Cabinet, also lacks insight into his moral dilemma and psychological motives. Towards the end of this novel Nimmo's character blurs; his loss of moral dynamism is not particularised. Through Nina, Cary asserts historical truisms about the causes of the post-war collapse of the Liberal Party—revulsion at its war policies, its internal schism, and the early post-war economic difficulties—but he gives little specification of Chester's personal decline.

In *Prisoner of Grace*, the rambling, parenthetical style of narration hinders Cary's strength in comically caricaturing minor figures. However, there is often a grotesque vigour in the presentation of Aunt Latter's brusque spinsterishness, Goold's moralistic censoriousness, Bootham's ponderous stupidity, and Daisy's self-indulgence. The characterisation of Nina's son, Tom, centres on the dilemma of reconciling freedom and order. Ironically, Nina believes the prevalent gossip that Chester crushed Tom by moral rigour. Yet in her compulsive self-revelation, Nina shows that she was more instrumental in Tom's suicide than Chester was, because she neglected to give moral guidance and encouraged her boy to follow the spurious freedom of fashionable permissiveness.

Nina needed freedom in order to gratify her needs. This novel shows that although she was attracted to Nimmo by a sense of his moral and rhetorical power, which Cary terms 'grace', she sometimes felt so desperate under Chester's moral imposition that she tried to commit suicide, then finally left him and married Jim Latter. Subsequently Chester shrewdly settled in with her and Jim, on the pretence of getting assistance for his memoirs. Nina loved Jim, but lied to him about her relationship with Nimmo and admitted only to herself this moral bond: 'I dare not turn Chester out. For I should know that I was committing a mean crime against something bigger than love.'[8] The book thus ends as it began, with the power of Chester's grace dominating but not displacing the force of Jim's love. This dichotomy between grace and sexual love is often presented ironically, because there is much egotism and lust in Nina's relationships. Nina tries to reconcile this conflict, but her attempts at suicide show the depth of her resultant stress and guilt.

Except the Lord is Chester Nimmo's account of his early life, when he resorted to Marxism as a means of rectifying social injustice, then became disillusioned and returned to Christian belief. Cary's title is from Psalm 127, which Chester quotes at the end of his account in order to indicate his spiritual revival in early manhood: 'Except the Lord build the house, their labour is but lost that build it; Except the Lord keep the city, the watchman waketh but in vain. Lo, children and the fruit of the womb are an heritage and gift that cometh of the Lord.'[9] The psalm warns man to remember God in his home and civic life, and asserts that children are God's reward. But in *Prisoner of Grace* Chester Nimmo often fell short of Christian ideals in politics and marriage, and was only blessed with children to the extent of claiming the paternity of Jim Latter's first two offspring by Nina. Nevertheless, Cary's irony towards Nimmo is sympathetic; the title of this novel is an expression of Nimmo's achievement as well as his failure.

Except the Lord is a mock-memoir in the Victorian convention, ostensibly written between the autumns of 1924–5 after Nimmo had visited his sister Georgina's grave on the moor. This visit recalled him to his childhood and young manhood—the years between the eighteen sixties and eighties in Devon. Chester Nimmo had experienced the cruel socio-economic forces which compelled most independent small-holders, such as his father, into the wage-earning classes. But Nimmo acquired from the yeoman tradition a knowledge and appreciation of the egalitarian and non-conformist values which inspired his ambition and ideals.

The beginning of *Except the Lord* is representative of Cary's technique of tonal contrast, which shows his moral perspective and ironic intention: 'If I draw back now the curtain from my family life, sacred to memory, I do so only to honour the dead, and in the conviction that my story throws light upon the crisis that so fearfully shakes our whole civilisation. It is the story of a crime, of a soul, my own, plucked back from the very edge of frustration and despair. I was a poor boy, brought up among the poorest in our moorland hamlet, itself a poor place. We had not always been so—the first six years of my life knew better things. My father then farmed Highfallow in Devonshire, forty acres on the moor. He was an independent yeoman under the Duchy.'[10] This passage appears to give essential facts, such as Chester's didactic literary intention and his poverty-stricken youth. But Nimmo's initial claim to be giving modern civilisation a lesson is exaggerated, and is thus given an ironic quality. Nimmo's rhetorical insistence and inflation—'so fearfully shakes', 'very edge', 'sacred to memory'—make these assertions dubious. But as Chester's memory engages with its subject more closely, the remembered facts, perceptions, and feelings are described with vividness and economy. The honest directness of the last two sentences in this passage is similar to the quality of the rest of the first chapter, and of other sections of the novel which are to be taken as reliable recollections.

In the first part of the novel Chester recalls the tension between joy and hardship when his family lived on their moorland farm. He specifies with imaginative freshness and vigour some of the pleasures which he had had during childhood: 'I see again the moors under snow and it is part of the joy that we are cut off, no one in the world can come to us; and all these great hills, these sphinx-like tors with their crowns of granite capped with ermine, couched about us like a guard of monsters extinct in all the world beside, drowse like the beasts of an older revelation upon the bed of winter.'[11] The specific nouns and verbs convey an original impression, and Chester's use of the present tense indicates his close recollection of the scene. This description does not contain the second-hand phrases, which Chester strung together for oratorical purposes in his later political life. His joy in nature is sincere, as are his descriptions of the love among his family, or of his parents' Christian compassion. But Nimmo also remembers injustice and hardship: the tuberculosis which killed his mother, the malice of neighbours who were envious of his mother's education and father's moral ideals, the bankruptcy which drove them off their own farm into labouring jobs. At this time Nimmo reconciled, through his Christian belief, the contradictions between the evil world and the ideal of love. Throughout most of this description of Nimmo's early childhood, Cary implies that the narration is reliable, because the expression is vivid and concise.

Nimmo was first torn between the moral absolutes of his father's Christianity, and a desire for worldly satisfactions, in the episode of the Lilmouth Great Fair, which he mentally associated with Bunyan's Vanity Fair. There Chester defied his puritan up-bringing, which taught that plays were lies, and attended *Maria Marten or The Murder in the Red Barn*—a Victorian melodrama about the seduction of a poor virgin by a rich villain. Nimmo recalls the effects of the play in arousing his moral feelings and social conscience. But he also candidly recounts his 'fascinated admiration' for Corder, the villain, and associates that sensation with the 'irresistible appeal' which Satan in Milton's *Paradise Lost* had for him: 'Is it fanciful in me to discover in Corder, that cut-throat of a booth drama, some tincture of the Lucifer who took upon himself all guilt and defied the very lightnings of Heaven? Or to find in that powerful experience of my young spirit some clue not only to that crime of which it is my purpose here to trace the source and nourishing, but even to the ruin and confusion which has fallen upon the world.'[12] In this crucial disclosure Nimmo's expression becomes increasingly inflated towards bombast. Chester's final moralistic phrase, which he repeats several times in the novel, is indicative of misdirection. Ironically, he associates the exciting temptation of rebelling against goodness with both his youthful rejection of God and the problems of post-First World War civilisation, but he refuses to notice the same theatrical tendency in his own career as a powerful Liberal politician. Yet Cary's presentation implies that this production of *Maria Marten* affected Nimmo's whole career, by showing him the way in which language and gesture could give the power to rouse both good and evil for political ends. What Chester dreams of at the end of his visit to the fair is not the content or quality of social revolution, but dramatic positions of power for himself: 'I was a king, a hero of the revolution.'[13] This vanity intruded continually into his later political life, as Nina unconsciously reveals in *Prisoner of Grace*, but he never completely submerged his ideals in rhetorical flourishes.

Christian charity is the outstanding quality of Chester's father, who is a lay preacher. But Tom Nimmo's prophecy of the

Second Coming is a pathetic comedy: 'It was raining—the dawn appeared like a dirty rag, and my father persisted in waiting for his Master until the little band of his personal followers, amounting to nine in all, including Mr. Newmarch, Edward G. and Fred Coyte, were so soaked and discouraged that Richard said loudly, "Nothing's going to happen now—it's nearly nine o'clock". My father turned on him and said, "Ah, Richard, for you it could never happen. Your eyes are blinded with the noise of disputation, and your ears are deaf with gazing on tales".'[14] The initial description is precise and graphic. Richard, Chester's brother, who later won a scholarship to Oxford, was sceptical of both religion and worldly goods. He here affronted his father, whose mixed metaphors are ludicrous. This dialogue humorously reveals Tom Nimmo's confusion about the meaning of the Second Coming, but it does not compromise Chester's respect for his father's goodness.

Through Nimmo's vividly dramatic narration, Cary specifies the social and physical oppression which led Chester, a fourteen-year-old farm labourer, to revolt into anarchism, and later, democratic socialism. Victimisation and other dangers finally drove him to Marxism, because he saw in its manifesto a persuasively argued programme of socio-political action, which seemed to promise creation out of destruction. But he was eventually motivated more by pride and lust for power, than by social conscience and a sense of justice. When he rose in the local Marxist leadership and helped to bring the Lilmouth dockers out on strike, he began to see the dishonesty and violent treachery in his revolutionary movement. However, Cary's presentation of Chester's moral and political development is sometimes inept: 'I say my heart was hardened. This is a true image if it is remembered that hearts are not metal but flesh. By work, by the blows of fate, the flesh can grow a surface as hard as horn, but not hard all through like steel. The cruel man need not have a hard heart. How many torturers, agents of despotism, experts with the rack and the thumb screw, have been tender fathers and loving husbands. The hard heart is that which turns aside the blows of truth, the arrows of conscience, and often it is hard above because it is soft and fearfully weak below.'[15] This metaphor is ludicrous and illogical. The narration becomes more confused as the comparison is elaborated into an apparent apology for torturers, rather than an indication of Nimmo's Marxist phase of confronting destructive injustices with destructive political action. The moral reason for Chester's retreat from being a powerful young Marxist demagogue, to being an evangelical Christian preacher during the next decade of his life, is not satisfactorily specified in this passage.

Georgina, Chester's beloved sister, integrated in her life the values of worldly vitality and moral ideals which he found so difficult to achieve. In concealing old Goold's sexual molestation of her, or in rejecting her father's prayers against her working in the beerhouse, she made practical compromises for the well-being of their motherless family. Despite her fiancé's offers to pay for treatment of her tuberculosis in a warm climate, she insisted on staying to care for her dying father and the rest of the family. The novel ends with Lord Nimmo recalling his visit to Georgina's grave the previous autumn: 'It was here, in the vast silence of the moor, that her spirit lived, silently awaiting me whether I came or no. I had come at last and my heart was beating again strongly to a heart that could not know despair because it forgot itself in the duty of its love. . . . "Here," I said, "the story began and here it shall begin again, in the things I lived with this forgotten one, in the young cruelty of the world, in the making of our souls."'[16] Chester movingly celebrates the love which Georgina had given her family continuously, as when she rescued him from probable violence in the street after his repudiation of the Marxist leaders. In making them a home Georgina had reconciled, but at tragic cost to herself, the demands of the world with the ideals of God. Chester at first wept over her grave, but then, as in Keats's letter about the world as a vale of soul-making, he joyfully re-asserted Georgina's faith in life.

Chester had nearly been destroyed body and soul by falling into political movements which excluded the spiritual and finally the moral. His father preached the rules of puritan asceticism and abstinence, but Tom Nimmo's family was preserved for him only because Georgina made vital compromises. Cary shows that she was happy because she was creative. In his narration Chester is at pains to demonstrate that his violent false start in politics taught him a life-long lesson which he had learnt fully, but which the civilisation of the nineteen twenties had not learnt. However, Cary, through his implicit commentary in *Prisoner of Grace* and *Not Honour More*, shows the irony of Chester's assurance that his later Liberalism, 'which inspired that great government in which I served',[17] was always a creative union of worldly concern and Christian ideal.

The title, *Not Honour More*, indicates the psychological and historical relationship in which Jim Latter, the narrator, stands to Chester Nimmo. The phrase, 'not honour more', is the conclusion to Richard Lovelace's 'To Lucasta, Going to the Wars' (1649). The last two stanzas of this three-stanza poem to a mistress are:

> True, a new mistress now I chase,
> The first foe in the field;
> And with a stronger faith embrace
> A sword, a horse, a shield.
>
> Yet this inconstancy is such
> As you too shall adore;
> I could not love thee, Dear, so much,
> Loved I not honour more.

Lovelace was a courtier of Charles I, and showed courage and loyalty fighting for his King in the Civil War against Cromwell. But Cromwell's New Model Army, which was inspired by the Protestant, egalitarian vision of a Commonwealth under God's justice, defeated the royalist cavaliers.

Cary's second trilogy has complex ironic associations with that period of English history. Captain James Latter sees himself as standing in descent from Colonel Lovelace, Sir John Suckling and those other gallants who tried to defend the order of the realm. But *Not Honour More* is an inversion of Lovelace's light witty poem. Latter's bitter defence of honour is ironically a sordid confession of hatred and murder, rather than a blithe assertion of the traditional gentlemanly verities. But with his unintended self-satire, Jim Latter also ridicules the corrupt side of Chester Nimmo—the inheritor of the non-conformist Christian tradition of Bunyan and Milton, who were the literary representatives of the puritan forces which defeated royalists such as Lovelace on the field. The modern political events with which this trilogy deals thus have historical depth in the imaginations of the main male characters.

Not Honour More (1955) is in the form of a policewoman's record of Jim Latter's confession before his trial on a charge of murder. The account contains Latter's eleventh-hour explanation and self-justification, which suggest the various strains and motives in his personality. The action of this novel is mainly the public and private responses of Chester Nimmo, Nina and Jim Latter to the General Strike of 1926, and the setting is Cary's imaginary Tarbiton-Queensport area in Devon. This last completed novel by Cary relates to his first novels, which are set in Africa. In Nigeria Jim Latter had been a 'pagan man'—a district officer who had protected his tribe, the Lugas, from material and social change. Nimmo and Latter's own family had exiled him there because of his sexual and financial peccadilloes, as Nina explains in *Prisoner of Grace*; however, Latter had made the Lugas the main concern of his life. Psychologically, Lugaland, unlike modern England, gave Latter a chance to feel as if he were a traditional gentleman—a respected and dignified squire protecting his people against exploitation and change.

Cary controls our response to Latter's narration by variations of expression. When Latter states facts and judgements which are reliable, he speaks with a restrained and often abbreviated expression, and Cary corroborates a few of these terse passages by similar information in the other two novels of the trilogy. But when Latter is deceiving himself and trying to deceive posterity, his expression is inflated. At the beginning of the novel Latter becomes repetitively insistent that he had always trusted his wife Nina, and that honour compelled him to try to shoot Lord Nimmo for 'interfering' with her: 'I say he spent his life destroying the country and selling the people. I say he corrupted everything and everybody that came near him and stole this woman, my wife, from me when she was little more than a child and set to work to destroy her body and soul. . . . I say it's the Nimmo gang who have destroyed all truth and honour in the country, including the sanctity of the home and marriage so that it is nothing but a jobber's match of gimme and what do I get out of it. . . . That's why I say I meant to kill this old evil man. . . .'[18] Latter quickly becomes more hysterical and defensive in this passage, repeating 'I say', and using banal clichés of thoughtless condemnation. Cary intends this mode of expression to be ironic, partly because in the other novels of this trilogy he convincingly presents some sympathetic aspects of Nimmo's character and political involvements. But the main clue to the irony of this tirade is Latter's self-deception about his marriage to Nina. In *Prisoner of Grace* Latter not only helped to break up Nimmo's marriage to her, but he had sexual relations with her repeatedly before and during that marriage, and sired both of Nimmo's children. Latter's claims to uphold traditional truth and honour against the lies and corruption of politicians such as Nimmo are thus grotesque. In fact, he hated egalitarians such as Nimmo because they were altering the traditional social hierarchy and thus the social basis of his psychological well-being.

Through his effective juxtaposition of inflated and reliable passages, Cary reveals Latter's character and the political history of the times. With a terse mockery which reflects his own bitterness and satirises Chester's moral compromises, Jim Latter recalls how Nimmo, while attempting a political comeback, had taken over the chairmanship of the Emergency Committee before the General Strike:

> Doors opened, crowd push and Nimmo comes upstairs
> on wave into council chamber on second floor, grinning
> all over face, skipping like sparrow. . . . Countess and
> wife in smartest new spring frocks. Bought for occasion,
> i.e. for any revolution on any side. Both smiling all
> round. Flushed with joy. Pushing out bosoms. . . . 'Let
> us adore him, the prophet of love.' Nimmo goes
> balcony with unemployed leader and Pincomb.
> Received with mixed noises like a dog fight. A lot of
> crowd saying 'To hell with the old wangler'. Poor
> aren't so mad. They've had a lot of talk before; they
> don't love the talky boys. And when he begins to
> speak, noise gets worse. No one can hear a word. In
> fact there aren't any. He just moves his mouth, saving
> celebrated voice. Smiles celebrated smile, waves
> celebrated arms. Yells of, 'Get out, Ches'. But not so
> many yells. And some people near bawling for silence.

> See his celebrated mouth moving, see him grinning,
> think they're missing something. In five minutes, a lot
> of them can hear word or two. 'Time for talk is past—
> the crisis is upon us. What's needed is action—at
> once—on largest most courageous lines. National works.
> To rebuild England. Money is there—only will wanting.
> And leadership. Let us go straight forward, with
> God's blessing.'[19]

Latter's satirical observations are abbreviated and plausible indications of the visible truth—how Nimmo used the citizenry, Nina and everyone else, by offering them what they wanted, whether it was employment, government subsidies or reflected glory. Latter is sarcastically aware of Nimmo's charisma for people like his wife, but he refuses to recognise that these people are Nimmo's accomplices in making representative democracy work. Cary's rendering of Latter's recollection humorously suggests the man's distaste for the untidiness of democracy, with its tolerance of 'noises like a dog fight' and 'talky boys'. Although Latter mockingly introduces Nimmo's platitudinous and partly hypocritical rhetoric, he also unconsciously shows that Nimmo has a more constructive approach than his own demand for the harsh enforcement of traditional order. Latter's narration catches the quality of Nimmo's public oratory much more evocatively than Nina's rambling and unspecific descriptions of it in *Prisoner of Grace*. Nimmo, like a good actor, knows how to husband his voice, involve the audience with him, appeal to patriotic and religious feelings, and use friendly gestures to imply good-will. Latter's summary conveys with economy and satiric humour the main features of Nimmo's rhetoric and the audience's response.

Because Latter was head of the special police during the General Strike, he knows accurately the duplicities and secret pacts of Chester and the Communist leaders. He convincingly condemns the turpitude of their political leadership, which promoted both the burning of a just owner's shipyard and the intimidation of innocent people. Nina was at the centre of this web of political and personal deceit. She served Nimmo loyally, but she was also tied to Latter by physical love. Cary is somewhat incoherent in Latter's account of Nina's rapid alterations; she wants to divorce Latter for interfering in her political intrigues, but at the same time she continually sleeps with him even after he caught Nimmo in her bed. Nina wanted to serve both men in order to fulfil her desires, but she would not allow either of them to strip her of dignity by forcing her to admit deception. Because of her ambiguous needs, these two jealous, possessive men were bound to cause impossible strains in her personality. But she did succeed once in assisting Nimmo to be a political power in the land, and she bore three children by Latter. Nina's final involvement in Nimmo's dream of a political comeback clashed disastrously with Latter's struggle to get justice for John Maufe, his junior special, who had been brought to court by the Communists on a charge of unjustified violence.

Cary shows Maufe's trial through the courtroom record and Latter's recollections. The Communist witnesses perjured themselves. After the strike the public also thought that Latter and his specials were militaristic cranks, rather than dutiful citizens who had saved Tarbiton and Lilmouth from revolutionary violence. The Communists' lawyer confused the evidence of Bell, the only honest witness, whom Nimmo had earlier suppressed in order to conform to left-wing sentiment against police violence, and to ensure his forthcoming opening with the Labour Party. Even after the court uncovered one of Nina's letters from Nimmo about Bell, Nina refused to divulge the truth and Maufe received a three-year prison sentence. Latter is a Kiplingesque figure; he sympathises with the brave, honest and dutiful underdogs who defend social institutions by their underpaid and unacknowledged efforts, but he scorns ordinary, undisciplined men. Sergeant Varney, who was crippled for life in the Communist-led violence at Potter's shipyard, and Maufe, are subjects whom Latter can admire and respond to with the same duty they show him. But Latter is intellectually and morally incapable of critically examining the social institutions which he upholds. This otherwise accomplished section of the novel is slightly marred by narrative confusion about whether the Pincomb incident was on 'the 9th' or 10th May.[20] Latter's dramatic account of this episode is corroborated by the trial record, so the contradiction must be Cary's lapse rather than a deliberate undermining of Latter's authoritativeness.

Cary concludes the novel with a grotesque scene of perverted justice and honour. Latter's search through Nina's correspondence, which proved the injustice done to Maufe by Nimmo and Nina, gave Latter the macabre excuse to avenge his humiliations in the name of truth. Nimmo fled from Latter and died of a heart attack in a locked toilet, but Latter killed Nina with his razor: 'I say I never loved this sweet woman so much as now when I knew she had to die. Because of the rottenness. Because of the corruption. Because all loyalty was a laugh and there was no more trust. Because marriage was turned into a skin game out of a nice time by safety first. Because of the word made dirt by hypocrites and cowards. Because there was no truth or justice anywhere any more. Because of the grabbers and tapeworms who were sucking the soul out of England.'[21] Latter's expression is once again aptly inflated and inaccurate—a parody of the feeling in Lovelace's poem. Cary thus indicates the irony of Latter's claim to be upholding honour and justice. Nimmo and Nina had committed an injustice, but he committed a greater one by murdering the mother of his young boy. Latter describes this killing as an 'execution' which he 'had to do', not 'just another sex crime'.[22] But his earlier attempts to kill Nimmo and Nina had been more because of jealous pride over Nina's unspecified sexual contact with Nimmo than because of their political compromises.

Cary's political trilogy is more interdependent in its realisation of character and theme than his Gulley Jimson trilogy. In the Jimson trilogy *To Be a Pilgrim* provides a necessary social and historical depth to the world of Gulley Jimson, but Wilcher's personal activities are almost completely separate from Jimson's actions. In the political trilogy, although Latter is not mentioned in *Except the Lord*, Nina, Chester Nimmo and Jim Latter are involved in many of the same personal and public events. The preceding discussion has indicated Cary's method of establishing the complex truth in his three narrations. Nina sees herself bound to the moral idealism and political career of Chester Nimmo, as well as to the physical love of Jim Latter, but many of her actions are ironically contrary to one or other of these fidelities. In *Except the Lord* Chester's compulsively exaggerated praise of Nina's moral purity is an ironic preparation for the tragic climax of *Not*

Honour More. Latter is jealous of Nina's first loyalty—Nimmo's vision—and when he discovers in her political activities the kind of deception which she has had to practise in order to preserve her relationships with both men, he kills her. In *Except the Lord* Nimmo's account of re-discovering in his early life the necessary moral basis of worldly endeavour shows that Nina is partly right to see him as a political visionary who is forced to compromise for the sake of democracy. But Latter's bitter narrative in *Not Honour More* mocks what Nina tries to excuse—Nimmo's tendency to rationalise his worldly compromises with hollow rhetoric, rather than to attain as near an approximation between political action and moral ideal as is possible in a democracy. Latter, as Nina observes in *Prisoner of Grace,* is brave and passionate, but in *Not Honour More* he reveals himself to be parroting at aristocratic conventions of honour and social order which are opposed to modern demands for freedom, as well as to many of his own actions. His bravery and passion are perverted into acts of hatred and finally murder.

Cary, unlike Yeats, Conrad and some other writers in the first part of the twentieth century, did *not* regret the passing of the old European traditions of a fairly rigid hierarchical social order and system of values. Cary's last trilogy does not prove the degeneracy of representative democracy, although human and institutional faults are effectively satirised in *Not Honour More.* Latter's condemnations of the workings of democracy are made persuasive by Cary's dramatic ability, but these attacks must be seen in connection with Latter's destructive personality, and in relation to the behaviour of Nimmo and Nina in the two earlier novels. As a politician, Nimmo is guilty of turpitude repeatedly, of pandering to ignorant public opinion, and of often failing to harmonise Christian ideals and political action, but he responds imaginatively to the problems of political life. Unlike Latter, he tries to be optimistically creative in the midst of political changes which are necessarily destructive of social institutions and values. Of course, this political trilogy is neither a defence of nor a programme for egalitarian democracy; Cary argued this case in political treatises such as *Power in Men.* Because the dramatic effectiveness of *Not Honour More* overshadows *Prisoner of Grace,* in which the authorial imposition of concepts and the narrative technique are often unsatisfactory, the moral and aesthetic focus of the trilogy is slightly blurred. But in his political trilogy Cary succeeds to a considerable extent in showing the dynamic conflicts within a few representative individuals and within the society of English democracy.

7 Cary's Achievement

Cary's short stories, the posthumously published novel, and his occasional pieces of expository prose contribute marginally to his achievement. The short story form, with its limited length, suited his skill in creating terse comic sketches of character and setting. The most satisfying stories in *Spring Song and Other Stories* (1960) were composed before the end of the Second World War, although not published in periodicals until later. Many of Cary's short stories are about children in relation to each other, to parents and old people, and to their domestic and natural surroundings. Cary developed Katherine Mansfield's technique of unfolding the small child's world through a few suggestive inside details. In stories such as 'A Special Occasion', 'Growing Up', 'A Hot Day', and 'New Boots', he conveys with humour, economy and originality his young characters' perceptions and feelings. He has an unsentimental understanding of the spontaneous cruelty and violence which coexist with innocence and joy in childhood.

In 'Spring Song' Cary integrates his natural setting with his characterisation of the two children: 'Spring in the park with an east wind and a sky as blue as winter milk. . . .'[1] The spring day reflects and heightens the pleasure of little Margaret and Tom, who dramatise their feelings by playing fantasy roles. Margaret enthusiastically invents a story in nonsense language, which annoys Gladys, their adolescent sister, '"It wasn't a dog—it was a singum—because—because—it came from Baffrica where all the dogs are scats." "Oh well, go on," with a sigh from the very heart of over-burdened teenage.'[2] Gladys, in contrast with the young children, feels the oppression of adult responsibility. The children's rejoicing with each other in imaginative language and gambols is an ironic comment on her self-conscious constraint. Although Gladys threatens to slap them for their exuberance, little Margaret has the last word as she picks up Vera, her discarded doll, 'Then she puts the doll into the perambulator and says in a low determined voice, "Lie down, Vera, or I'll give you such a smack on your poly".'[3] Margaret's action and words, which implicitly mock Gladys's threatening insistence on convention at the expense of freedom, are a comically apt conclusion to a delightful story.

In many of his stories, Cary examines the way a child establishes moral truth by imaginative trial. Moore, in 'A Hero of Our Time', is brought to realise that his violent imaginings, if made real, would be disastrous to his well-being. He mixes chemicals from his older brother's chemistry set, then leaves the house in the hope of seeing the place 'blow up'. But when Richard, his friend, reiterates that the house will also 'fall down' on his mother, Moore quickly disavows violence and declares that the visible smoke is from the chimney, not from an explosion: 'He gave a thoughtful solemn skip, then ran forward, throwing out his legs in a proud manner, and pushing forward his stomach. He was pleased with himself. He had saved his mother's life.'[4] Cary's irony is directed against Moore's earlier violent whimsy, and it humorously shows the boy's imaginative realisation of the importance of family love.

The most accomplished of Cary's short stories about life in colonial Nigeria is 'Bush River', which is partly autobiographical. This story centres on the characterisation of its hero, Captain Corner, who swims a spirited Barbary stallion, Satan, across an African river during the First World War campaign against the German Cameroons. Cary shows the tension between Corner's determination and the mutinous feelings of his soldiers, who fear the deep river, the Germans, and the evil spirits of the place. Corner, whose sensibility is heightened by this emotional atmosphere, welcomes the opportunity to overcome difficult obstacles and discover himself. After narrow escapes from drowning and being shot by a German soldier, he is brought to this conclusion: 'He turned his thought from the event, from Satan—he would not even look at the river. But all the more, they were present to his feeling, the feeling of one appointed to a special fate, to gratitude.'[5] The central image of this story—swimming a powerful horse across a dangerous river—is similar to motifs in *The*

African Witch, some of D. H. Lawrence's fiction, and other literature and mythology in which an explosive energy is harnessed and a divide in the development of the personality is crossed. In 'Bush River', Cary's concise and vivid use of this image suggests Corner's realisation of a new area of his character. Corner, a *persona* for Cary himself, is determined to reach the far bank of the river by harnessing his courage and will to his energy and emotions. But he finds that he is saved by a 'special fate' which is grace.

Cary's unfinished manuscript of *The Captive and the Free* (1959) was sympathetically edited by Winifred Davin, one of his friends, but the published novel required some editorial guess-work and interpolations.[6] The manuscript of this novel lacks a few important episodes, and Cary would probably have cut or changed several infelicitous and contradictory passages. It is unfair to criticise this unsatisfactory work because, in a strict sense, it is not part of Cary's canon. From the title onwards, the binary system of his metaphysics is often imposed on, rather than made integral to, the action. But the incongruous conflicts between belief and truth in the lives of two clergymen, a journalist and their gullible audiences are sometimes forcefully specified.

Cary wrote a considerable amount of occasional prose on politics and social questions. The most substantial of this writing is *Power in Men* (1939) for the Liberal Book Club, and *The Case for African Freedom* (1941; revised 1944) for George Orwell's Searchlight Series. *Power in Men* is a statement of Cary's political and moral principles—an assertion of metaphysical beliefs rather than of rigorous logic. His political position had evolved by 1939 from the idea of freedom as an absence of restraint, to the ideal that freedom is a field of creative power which must be preserved and extended by education, health, economic prosperity and a pluralism of interest groups. However, *Power in Men* tends to be contradictory in claiming that moral freedom is man's absolute condition, that intellectual freedom is always variable, and that political freedom, as referred to in this peroration, expands constantly: 'Those who fight liberty set themselves against a power more subtle than thought; as secret as will; as persistent as nature, of which it is the life; as all-pervading as life, of which it is spirit; at a time when, throughout all countries of the world, it swells up towards the last phase of its revolutionary triumphs and the first of its world mastery.'[7] Cary's derivatively Marxist inflation of style in this conclusion and elsewhere in the treatise also blurs his actual awareness of the dangers to political freedom.

The Case for African Freedom (revised 1944) is a much more satisfactory work than *Power in Men*, because Cary's argument for African freedom rests on cogently expressed observations rather than on speculation. In *Joyce Cary's Africa* Professor Mahood argues that Cary's case is dated because it has been won. In fact, the crux of Cary's prospectus for African freedom is economic development, and those Africans who write on the present problems of achieving real freedom in their countries do not differ markedly from his insight. Cary's many short articles on political and social questions develop variations on his theme of creative freedom, which, paradoxically, both derives from and increases functional democracy. Errors of fact and logic occur in these essays, but Cary almost invariably shows goodwill and liberal beliefs, as in this comment from 'Britain and West Africa' (1946) about the effects of positive freedom. 'There is no fear that tropical Africa will lose its local qualities when it is permitted to take its place in the world; rather it will bring to the world a new African civilisation, new arts, new religion.'[8] The ideals in Cary's essays are variously implicit or explicit in all his novels.

Art and Reality (1958), which Cary prepared for the 1956 Clark Lectures at Cambridge, is a series of reflections on aesthetic theory and the practice of art. Much of the material which Cary had recorded previously in articles and interviews[9] about the art of fiction is integrated into this work. His analysis of theoretical aesthetics, which he bases on a partial refutation of Croce, is confusing because of his inconsistent use of fundamental terms such as 'intuition', 'idea', 'fact', 'feeling', 'theme', 'concept', and 'meaning'. But Cary's practical discussion of symbolism in art is a sensible departure from critical and psychological jargon. He identifies, for example, the actual associations of Winston Churchill's cigar, and the significance of the violent riding scene in D. H. Lawrence's *St. Mawr* (1925), with the shrewd insight of an artist who had once been a political officer and horseman. Cary enjoyed theorising, but his prose in *Art and Reality* has much more strength and penetration when it stems from his observations of life and his experience of writing.

Cary's practical criticism of novelists such as D. H. Lawrence is pertinent and illuminating. In illustrating what he believed to be the most fundamental artistic task—unifying intuition (fundamental feelings and perceptions) with moral concepts and traditional associations—Cary explicates the christening scene in Hardy's *Tess of the d'Urbervilles* (1891), 'He shows Tess as responsible for the child's soul, and he shows it in a dramatic form. He renews for us also the christening service, because it is Tess, the mother, with all her obsessive anxiety for that child's salvation, who performs it. He adds to the dramatic intensity of the situation all the weight of dramatic ritual as it lies in our recollection.'[10] This observation not only shows Hardy's method of symbolic realism, but also implies one aspect of Cary's intention in his own novels. In addition to *Art and Reality*, many of Cary's essays, such as the prefaces to his novels, and the 'Introduction' (1958) to R. S. Surtees's *Mr. Sponge's Sporting Tour* (1853), provide hints about his sources of technique and form—for example, comic dialogue and caricature in Surtees and Dickens, and the use of mythic patterns of imagery in Hardy, D. H. Lawrence and Conrad. Several details of content in Cary's fiction stem from the personal experiences which he relates in his lively autobiographical essays; for example, 'Barney Magonagel' and 'Cromwell House' refer to parts of Cary's family history which he used in *Castle Corner* and *A House of Children*, and 'The Most Exciting Sport in the World' recounts a sporting experience which supplied the polo-playing scene in *The African Witch*.

The reviewers' responses to Cary's novels varied; his best novels received polite admiration in some British dailies, and, when published much later in America, attracted enthusiastic praise in several serious publications there. But in established literary periodicals in Britain, reviews of his novels were often uncomprehending and disparaging. The anonymous *TLS* reviewer of *The Horse's Mouth* (1944) wrote, '. . . it is, all things considered, portentously trifling in content and monotonous and fatiguing to read. . . . it is a pity he seems so deeply concerned to demonstrate how very experimental he can be.'[11] Some reviewers in the *TLS* and elsewhere complained, as many reviewers had once complained of D. H. Lawrence, that even Cary's most accomplished fiction lacks moral focus. In 1957 Martin Seymour-Smith in *Encounter* still took the view that Cary's novels lack 'moral conflict' and therefore 'do not demand serious critical attention'.[12] However, several reviewers, notably Walter Allen, Saul Bellow (in America), and V. S. Pritchett, wrote laudatory reviews[13] which illuminate Cary's varied content and expression.

Since Cary's death in 1957 some scholarly criticism of his novels has been published. Andrew Wright's *Joyce Cary: A Preface to His Novels* (1958) mainly expands what Cary wrote in his own prefaces and other essays about the metaphysical ideas behind his novels. Almost all the later books on Cary's work by academic critics[14] take up Wright's misleading preoccupation with this component of his fiction and neglect to evaluate his novels as literary art. Cary's metaphysical elaborations on freedom and other ideas are flawed in his essays, and are not the foremost feature of his most satisfying novels. His strength lay in transmuting his vision of life into art. From this standpoint M. M. Mahood's *Joyce Cary's Africa* (1964) is a valid and stimulating biographical critique of Cary's African novels. Malcolm Foster's *Joyce Cary: A Biography* (1968) is an informative chronicle of Cary's life, but his accompanying criticism and history have several errors of fact in matters such as details of plots and the causes of British intrusion into West Africa.

Cary's basic metaphysical ideas—that creative activity is the reason for and fulfilment of life, and that moral and political freedom is the necessary milieu for creativity—are implicit in his best novels and explicit in his least satisfactory. He is an artist who is most successful in works in which the coherent and original expression of true perceptions, emotions and sensations subsumes the communication of metaphysical truths. His novels, like Blake's poetry, were intended to cohere in an integrated formulation of his vision of life. In *Mister Johnson* (1939), a creative individual and dynamic setting are presented with freshness and insight. Among Cary's earlier African novels, only *An American Visitor* (1933), despite limitations in the characterisation of Africans, is partially comparable to *Mister Johnson* in the achievement of aesthetic form, moral coherence and verbal felicity.

Cary's first trilogy—*Herself Surprised* (1941), *To Be a Pilgrim*

(1942), and *The Horse's Mouth* (1944)—is his greatest achievement. He succeeds in showing the multiplicity of life by dramatising the feelings and perceptions of each character in turn, yet at the same time he controls the moral and aesthetic focus of the whole by variations of expression, ironic contrasts and patterns of imagery. His integrated use of methods as varied as mock-autobiography and stream-of-consciousness narration shows a wide range of skills and imaginative facility. He reveals the comedy of freedom through the lives of a cook, lawyer and artist—both the inner world of each protagonist and the outside society.

A few of Cary's other works, although not as comprehensive or original as the Gulley Jimson trilogy, are important achievements. *A House of Children* (1941) and several stories such as 'Spring Song' show Cary's ability to delineate children's perceptions and emotions. His expression in these works has lyricism and economy, and his form suggests a free continuum which is the child's world. *The Moonlight* (1946), despite occasional ineptness of expression, convincingly portrays the dynamic historical and natural forces within and around two generations of women.

The remainder of Cary's work is uneven in quality, and some of it has fundamental defects of craftsmanship. But he continued to extend his range of content and expression until the end of his life. His last completed work, the political trilogy (*Prisoner of Grace*, *Except the Lord*, and *Not Honour More*, 1952–55), develops the form of his first trilogy in order to set forth the politics of public and private life during the last expansive phase of British history. This subject tempted Cary, especially in *Prisoner of Grace*, to indulge in the kind of detached political and historical speculation which mars works such as *Castle Corner*. However, both *Prisoner of Grace* and *Not Honour More* have original departures in technique—the ineffective experiment with qualification by brackets in the former novel, and the satisfactory technique of a recorded confession to the police in the latter. *Not Honour More*, aside from some minor carelessness about details, is a remarkable dramatisation of a twentieth-century Englishman who despised the age.

Even from this near point in time, it is clear that Cary has extended the limits of English fiction. Anthony Burgess points out, with regard to the influence of Cary's African novels in Africa, E. M. Forster's *A Passage to India* (1924) in India, and D. H.

Lawrence's *Kangaroo* (1923) in Australia, '. . . these are accepted as modern classics. They may also be regarded as the creators of whole new national literatures in English.'[15] Burgess exaggerates in his use of the term 'creators', and probably intends 'precursors'. Nevertheless, Chinua Achebe, the West African writer, has several times paid credit to Cary as the main written stimulus to his own work as a novelist: '*Mister Johnson*, he says, was precisely *the* book that made all the difference. It was the provocation, and the watershed. He would have disregarded an Edgar Wallace, but Cary was good, he was sympathetic, he knew Africa.'[16] To recent West African writers, even if, like Achebe, they disagree with some of Cary's perceptions, Cary made the written tradition of the English novel pertinent by showing that it is an adaptable artistic form for exploring and projecting African reality. In *Mister Johnson*, and to a considerable extent in his earlier African novels, Cary broke free of the biases and stereotypes which had dominated the fiction of earlier writers, such as G. A. Henty and Edgar Wallace, who had sometimes used West Africa as an exotic setting. Cary thus opened up a new geographical and cultural area for fiction in English.

Cary also extended the formal tradition of English fiction in his trilogies, which renewed and synthesised various techniques such as mock-autobiography. Saul Bellow, the American novelist, implies that Cary's contribution to modern fiction, especially in revitalising the comic forms of the early tradition of the English novel, is an invigorating example: 'He is one of the most dexterous novelists now writing, with an enviable command of styles and a truly original point of view.'[17] In the *Alexandria Quartet* (1956–60) Lawrence Durrell seems to have employed Cary's innovation by presenting four protagonists who respectively narrate their partially coincidental lives. Although Durrell uses experimental expression, which is more related to Faulkner than Cary, in order to convey a sense of timelessness throughout his quartet, there is some affinity between Durrell's multiple novels and Cary's original form of trilogy. But Cary's influence on the subsequent form and content of the novel in English is subsidiary to the achievement of his most satisfying novels—creating a vision of life which is original, entertaining, morally penetrating and aesthetically coherent.

References

Chapter 1

1. MS. Letter, Cary to Mark Schorer, 1951, Osborn Collection.
2. William Blake, *Complete Writings*, ed. Keynes, 1966, p. 776.
3. William Blake, p. 604.
4. 'Cromwell House', *The New Yorker*, Nov. 3 1956, p. 67.
5. MS. Notebook, Osborn Collection.
6. MS. Letter, Cary to His Wife, 1917, Osborn Collection.
7. *C.A.F.*, p. 133.
8. *C.A.F.*, p. 38.
9. MS. Letter, Cary to His Wife, 1919, Osborn Collection.
10. *C.A.F.*, p. 24.
11. MS., 'The Split Mind of the West,' Osborn Collection.

Chapter 2

1. *A.S.*, p. 11.
2. *A.S.*, p. 30.
3. *A.S.*, p. 34.
4. *A.S.*, pp. 153–4.
5. *A.S.*, p. 195.
6. *A.S.*, p. 211.
7. *A.S.*, p. 211.
8. MS. Letter, Cary to Ernest Benn, Osborn Collection.
9. *A.V.*, p. 127.
10. *A.V.*, p. 66.
11. *A.V.*, p. 237.
12. *A.V.*, p. 238.
13. *A.V.*, p. 66.
14. *A.V.*, pp. 24–5.
15. *A.V.*, pp. 193–4.

16. *A.R.*, pp. 158–9.
17. *A.W.*, pp. 42–3.
18. *A.W.*, pp. 53–4.
19. *A.W.*, p. 308.
20. *A.W.*, pp. 72–3.
21. *A.W.*, p. 87–9.
22. *A.W.*, pp. 99–103.
23. *A.W.*, pp. 148–9.
24. *C.A.F.*, p. 102.
25. *C.C.*, p. 7.
26. *C.C.*, p. 8.
27. *C.C.*, p. 9.
28. *C.C.*, p. 15.
29. *C.C.*, p. 75.
30. *C.C.*, p. 91.
31. *C.C.*, p. 40.
32. *C.C.*, p. 51.
33. *C.C.*, p. 372.
34. *M.J.*, pp. 27–8.
35. *M.J.*, p. 106.
36. *M.J.*, p. 130.
37. *M.J.*, p. 227.
38. *M.J.*, pp. 14–15.
39. *M.J.*, p. 99.
40. *M.J.*, p. 105.
41. MS. Letter, Cary to His Wife, Osborn Collection.
42. *M.J.*, p. 149.
43. *M.J.*, p. 162.
44. *M.J.*, p. 163.
45. *M.J.*, p. 221.

Chapter 3

1. *C.I.M.D.*, pp. 38–9.
2. *C.I.M.D.*, pp. 48–9.
3. *C.I.M.D.*, pp. 128–30.
4. *C.I.M.D.*, p. 131.

5. *C.I.M.D.*, p. 144.
6. *C.I.M.D.*, p. 217.
7. *C.I.M.D.*, p. 302.
8. *C.I.M.D.*, p. 325.
9. *C.I.M.D.*, p. 329.
10. *H.C.*, p. 9.
11. *H.C.*, p. 53.
12. *H.C.*, p. 115.
13. *H.C.*, pp. 173-4.
14. *H.C.*, p. 234.
15. *H.C.*, p. 239.

Chapter 4

1. *H.S.*, p. 9.
2. *H.S.*, p. 13.
3. *H.S.*, pp. 30-1.
4. *H.S.*, pp. 92-3.
5. *H.S.*, p. 143.
6. *H.S.*, p. 220.
7. *B.P.*, p. 14.
8. *B.P.*, p. 15.
9. *B.P.*, p. 16.
10. *B.P.*, p. 39.
11. *B.P.*, p. 154.
12. *B.P.*, p. 128.
13. *B.P.*, p. 328.
14. *B.P.*, pp. 341-2.
15. *H.M.*, p. 11.
16. *H.M.*, p. 26.
17. *H.M.*, pp. 52-3.
18. *H.M.*, p. 62.
19. *H.M.*, p. 100.
20. *H. M.*, p. 211.
21. *H.M.*, p. 225.
22. e.g., *The Times Literary Supplement* Sept. 9 1944, p. 437.

Chapter 5

1. *M.*, p. 9.
2. *M.*, p. 18.
3. *M.*, pp. 233–4.
4. *M.*, p. 68.
5. *M.*, p. 150.
6. *M.*, p. 217.
7. *M.*, pp. 314–15.
8. *M.*, p. 251.
9. *M.*, p. 300.
10. *F.J.*, p. 6.
11. *F.J.*, p. 19.
12. *F.J.*, p. 23.
13. *F.J.*, p. 41.
14. *F.J.*, p. 77.
15. *F.J.*, p. 356.
16. *F.J.*, p. 388.

Chapter 6

1. *P.G.*, p. 230.
2. *P.G.*, p. 9.
3. *P.G.*, p. 215.
4. *P.G.*, p. 26.
5. *P.G.*, p. 85.
6. *P.G.*, p. 92.
7. *P.G.*, p. 214.
8. *P.G.*, p. 402.
9. *E.L.*, p. 284.
10. *E.L.*, p. 5.
11. *E.L.*, p. 7.
12. *E.L.*, p. 94.
13. *E.L.*, p. 100.
14. *E.L.*, pp. 120–1.
15. *E.L.*, p. 268.

16. *E.L.*, p. 287.
17. *E.L.*, p. 276.
18. *N.H.M.*, pp. 8–9.
19. *N.H.M.*, pp. 16–17.
20. *N.H.M.*, pp. 200, 207, 154–7.
21. *N.H.M.*, p. 220.
22. *N.H.M.*, p. 223.

Chapter 7

1. *S.S.*, p. 55.
2. *S.S.*, p. 56.
3. *S.S.*, p. 57.
4. *S.S.*, p. 180.
5. *S.S.*, p. 18.
6. MS., *The Captive and the Free*, Osborn Collection.
7. *P.M.*, p. 243.
8. *C.A.F.*, p. 195.
9. e.g., *Adam International Review* (Joyce Cary issue), Nov.–Dec. 1950, pp. 1–11, 15–25.
10. *A. R.*, p. 172.
11. *The Times Literary Supplement*, Sept. 9 1944, p. 437.
12. *Encounter*, Nov. 1957, pp. 38–51.
13. Walter Allen's reviews are expanded in his British Council pamphlet, *Joyce Cary*, rev. 1963; Saul Bellow in *New Republic*, Feb. 22 1954, pp. 20–1; V. S. Pritchett in *New Statesman*, Oct. 27 1951, pp. 464–5.
14. e.g., Robert Bloom, *The Indeterminate World: A Study of the Novels of Joyce Cary*, 1962; Golden C. Larsen, *The Dark Descent: Social Change and Moral Responsibility in the Novels of Joyce Cary*, 1965.
15. Anthony Burgess, *The Novel Now*, New ed. 1971, p. 156.
16. Report of an Interview with Chinua Achebe, *Guardian*, Feb. 28 1972, p. 8.
17. *New Republic*, Feb. 22 1954, p. 20.

Bibliography

Note—The following select bibliography is based partly on I. R. Willison's lists of primary and secondary materials in the Joyce Cary section of his *New Cambridge Bibliography of English Literature, Vol. IV, 1900–1950*, Cambridge (C.U.P.), 1972; and Barbara Fisher's 'Joyce Cary's Published Writings' in *Bodleian Library Record*, 8, 1970, pp. 213–28. The James M. Osborn collection in the Bodleian Library, Oxford, contains nearly all of Joyce Cary's manuscripts. References in my study of Cary are taken from the most authoritative available editions, which are marked * in the following list. Cary's only work for which a slightly more authoritative edition was prepared is *The Horse's Mouth*, in the Rainbird Edition and *First Trilogy*, but this edition is not in print in Britain.

1   Joyce Cary

(a) Novels and Collected Short Stories

Aissa Saved. London (Ernest Benn) 1932. New York (Harper) 1962. * Carfax edn., London (Michael Joseph) 1952.
An American Visitor. London (Ernest Benn) 1933. New York (Harper) 1961. * Carfax edn., London (Michael Joseph) 1952.
The African Witch. London (Victor Gollancz) and New York (William Morrow) 1936. * Carfax edn., London (Michael Joseph) 1951.
Castle Corner. London (Victor Gollancz) 1938. New York (Harper) 1963. * Carfax edn., London (Michael Joseph) 1952.
Mister Johnson. London (Victor Gollancz) 1939. New York (Harper) 1951. * Carfax edn., London (Michael Joseph) 1952.

Charley Is My Darling. London (Michael Joseph) 1940. New York (Harper) 1960. * Carfax edn., London (Michael Joseph) 1951.

A House of Children. London (Michael Joseph) 1941. New York (Harper) 1956. * Carfax edn., London (Michael Joseph) 1951.

Herself Surprised. London (Michael Joseph) 1941. New York (Harper) 1948. * Carfax edn., London (Michael Joseph) 1951.

To Be a Pilgrim. London (Michael Joseph) 1942. New York (Harper) 1949. * Carfax edn., London (Michael Joseph) 1951.

The Horse's Mouth. London (Michael Joseph) 1944. New York (Harper) 1950. * Carfax edn., London (Michael Joseph) 1951. Rev. Rainbird edn. with Cary's illustrations and a discarded ch., 'The Old Strife at Plant's', London (Michael Joseph) 1957. Rev. edn. reprinted with *Herself Surprised* and *To Be a Pilgrim*, in *First Trilogy*, New York (Harper) 1958.

The Moonlight. London (Michael Joseph) 1946. New York (Harper) 1947. * Carfax edn., London (Michael Joseph) 1952.

A Fearful Joy. London (Michael Joseph) 1949. New York (Harper) 1950. * Carfax edn., London (Michael Joseph) 1952.

Prisoner of Grace. London (Michael Joseph) and New York (Harper) 1952. * Carfax edn., London (Michael Joseph) 1954.

Except the Lord. New York (Harper) and * London (Michael Joseph) 1953.

Not Honour More. London (Michael Joseph) and New York (Harper) 1955. * Carfax edn., London (Michael Joseph) 1966.

The Captive and the Free. New York (Harper) and London (Michael Joseph) 1959. * Carfax edn., London (Michael Joseph) 1963.

Spring Song and Other Stories. * London (Michael Joseph) and New York (Harper) 1960.

(b) Expository Prose Works

Power in Men. London (Nicholson & Watson for the Liberal Book Club) 1939. * Seattle (Univ. of Washington) 1963.

The Case for African Freedom. London (Secker & Warburg) 1941. Rev. edn. 1944. * Reprinted with Cary's other essays about

Africa in *The Case for African Freedom and Other Writings on Africa,* Austin (Univ. of Texas) 1962.

Art and Reality. * Cambridge (Cambridge Univ. Press) and New York (Harper) 1958.

Memoir of the Bobotes. Austin (Univ. of Texas) 1960. * London (Michael Joseph), 1964.

(c) Miscellaneous

Cary had many essays and three booklets of verse published. The following essays are the most substantial pieces of this occasional writing.

'Tolstoy's Theory of Art', in *Univ. of Edinburgh Journal,* XII, Summer, 1943, pp. 91–6.

Process of Real Freedom. London (Michael Joseph) 1943.

'The Way a Novel Gets Written', in *Harper's Magazine,* cc, Feb. 1950, pp. 87–93; reprinted in * *Adam International Review,* XVIII, Nov.–Dec. 1950, pp. 3–11.

'What Does Art Create', in *Literature and Life,* II, Addresses to the English Association, London (Harrap) 1951, pp. 32–45.

'The Front-Line Feeling', in *The Listener,* Jan. 17 1952, pp. 92–3.

'The Period Novel', in *The Spectator,* Nov. 21 1952, p. 684.

'Barney Magonagel', in *The New Yorker,* June 19 1954, pp. 27–31.

'A Novelist and His Public', in *The Listener,* Sept. 30 1954, pp. 521–2; reprinted in *Saturday Review,* November 27 1954, pp. 11, 36, 37.

'Political and Personal Morality', in *Saturday Review,* Dec. 31 1955, pp. 5, 6, 31, 32.

'Cromwell House', in *The New Yorker,* Nov. 3 1956, pp. 45–67.

'The Tough World of Surtees', in *The Sunday Times,* April 14 1957, p. 8; reprinted as * 'Introduction' to R. S. Surtees's *Mr. Sponge's Sporting Tour.* Worlds Classics edn., London (Oxford Univ. Press) 1958, pp. vii–xii.

'The Most Exciting Sport in the World', in *Holiday,* XXI, June 1957, pp. 42, 44, 47–8, 155, 157.

2   Others

The following items are a recommended selection.

ALLEN, WALTER: *Joyce Cary*, Rev. edn., London, 1963.

BURROWS, J., and HAMILTON, A.: Interview with Joyce Cary in *The Paris Review*, 7, 1954. Reprinted in * *Writers at Work*, ed. Malcolm Cowley, London, 1958, pp. 47–61.

CECIL, DAVID: Interview with Joyce Cary in *Adam International Review*, XVIII, Nov.–Dec. 1950, pp. 15–25.

COHEN, NATHAN: Interview with Joyce Cary in *Tamarack Review*, 3, Spring, 1957, pp. 5–15.

FOSTER, MALCOLM: *Joyce Cary: A Biography*, Boston, 1968.

HARDY, BARBARA: 'Form in Joyce Cary's Novels', in *Essays in Criticism*, IV, Oct. 1954, pp. 180–90.

HOFFMAN, CHARLES G., *Joyce Cary: The Comedy of Freedom*, Pittsburgh, 1964.

HOLLOWAY, JOHN: 'Joyce Cary's Fiction: Modernity and Sustaining Power', in *TLS*, Aug. 7 1959, pp. XIV–XV; reprinted in *The Colours of Clarity*, London, 1964.

MAHOOD, M. M.: *Joyce Cary's Africa*, London, 1964.

WRIGHT, ANDREW: *Joyce Cary: A Preface to His Novels*, London, 1958.